DATE DUE FOR RETURN

Tough Topics

Peer Pressure

Elizabeth Raum

www.heinemann.co.uk/library
Visit our website to find out more information about Heinemann Library books.

To order:
 Phone 44 (0) 1865 888066
 Send a fax to 44 (0) 1865 314091
 Visit the Heinemann Bookshop at www.heinemann.co.uk/library to browse our catalogue and order online.

First published in Great Britain by Heinemann Library, Halley Court, Jordan Hill, Oxford OX2 8EJ, part of Harcourt Education.
Heinemann is a registered trademark of Harcourt Education Ltd.

Editorial: Rebecca Rissman and Diyan Leake
Design: Joanna Hinton-Malivoire
Picture research: Tracy Cummins and Heather Mauldin
Production: Duncan Gilbert

Origination: Dot Gradations Ltd
Printed and bound in China by South China Printing Co. Ltd

ISBN 978 0 431 90829 8
12 11 10 09 08
10 9 8 7 6 5 4 3 2 1

British Library Cataloguing in Publication Data
Raum, Elizabeth
Peer Pressure
    303.3'27

A full catalogue record for this book is available from the British Library.

Acknowledgments
The author and publisher are grateful to the following for permission to reproduce copyright material: © Corbis pp. 4 (Don Mason), 9 (zefa/Heide Benser), 13 (zefa/Emely), 26 (Hill Street/Studios/StockThisWay); © Getty Images pp. 5 (Simon Watson), 6 (Sean Justice), 7 (Leland Bobbe), 8 (Laurence Moulton), 10 (Ned Frisk), 11 (Ruth Jenkinson), 12 (Stockbyte), 14, 15, 20, 24, 28, 29 (Royalty Free), 16 (Digital Vision), 17 (Lisa Peardon), 18 (Matt Henry Gunther), 21 (LWA/Dann Tardif), 22 (Camille Tokerud), 23 (Peter Cade), 25 (Andreas Kuehn), 27 (Richard Koek).

Cover photograph reproduced with permission of © Corbis/Thinkstock.

Every effort has been made to contact copyright holders of any material reproduced in this book. Any omissions will be rectified in subsequent printings if notice is given to the publisher.

The author would like to thank Ms Helen Scully, Guidance Counselor, Central Elementary School, Warren Township, New Jersey, USA for her valuable assistance.

Contents

Some words are shown in bold, **like this**. You can find out what they mean by looking in the glossary.

What is peer pressure?

People who are about the same age or in the same year at school are called **peers**. Sometimes our peers are our friends. Children have friends, and so do adults. Everyone enjoys spending time with friends.

▲These peers are having fun at a picnic together.

▼It can be fun to do what our peers do.

When we do things because our peers tell us to, it is called **peer pressure**. When we do things because we want to be part of a group, that's peer pressure, too. Many children do things because they want others to like them.

▲It feels great when peers cheer for you.

Sometimes peer pressure can be good. It is fun to be part of a team or a club. Peers on sports teams may **encourage** us to practise and try harder. Peers in clubs often work together to help others.

Peers may encourage us to study harder. Peers may ask us to join a music group or take an art class. Peers who want to make the world a better place encourage us to be kind and helpful.

▲These peers work together to help the environment.

Sometimes peer pressure is bad. It's bad when a peer puts pressure on us to do things we would not do on our own. Sometimes a peer puts pressure on us to be unkind to others or to do things that are unsafe or **harmful**.

◄ These peers are being unkind.

▲ No one wants to be left out.

Groups use peer pressure, too. Some groups leave certain children out or spread **gossip**. Groups of peers can gang up on others.

Why do I feel peer pressure?

You may feel caught between what your peers want you to do and what you know is the right thing to do. Sometimes what your peers want to do is not bad, but it's not right for you. It's hard to say, "No."

▶ It's important to think about what is right for you.

▲ It's not easy to say,
"No," to your peers.

Most children enjoy being part of a group. Some children are afraid that others will make fun of them or laugh at them if they don't go along with the group. It's not always easy to stand up for yourself and do the right thing.

What can I do when I feel peer pressure?

The next time your peers ask you to do something, don't say, "Yes", right away. Take a minute to decide what is right for you. Making a good **decision** is difficult. But you can do it.

▲Stop and think before you say, "Yes."

Ask yourself: "Is this something I want to do? Is this something my parents want me to do? Is it safe? Is it against the rules? Is it kind?"

◄ You can make difficult decisions.

▲These girls made a good choice to play together on the playground.

If you feel sure that what your peers want you to do is a good idea, then do it and have fun. But if it doesn't feel right, don't do it. It's better to say, "No", than to go along with the group.

▼When you make good choices, you can feel proud of yourself.

Remember that you are in charge of what you do. You are a strong person with good ideas. Do what you know is best for you.

▲ If your friends make you feel left out,
find new friends who will be kind to you.

It's okay if some people don't like you.
It's more important to make wise
choices than to be friends with everyone.
Your choices make a difference in your
life and the lives of others.

Tell yourself that you need friends who **respect** the choices you make. Good friends understand that sometimes you have to say, "No." Good friends accept you the way you are.

▲Good friends understand your choices.

How do I say, "No"?

◄ Be friendly and sure of yourself. People will know they cannot put pressure on you.

There are lots of ways to say, "No." Make sure you let others know that you mean what you say. Stand up straight, smile, and say, "No."

Tell the truth. Don't be afraid to say, "My parents won't let me" or "It's against the rules." Whatever you say, make sure to say it clearly and then walk away.

How to Say, "No"

You might say:

- No, but maybe another time.
- No way, let's do something else.
- No, I don't want to.
- No, it isn't nice.
- No, it's not safe.
- No, my parents won't let me.

Choose friends wisely

If your friends put too much pressure on you, make new friends. You might find new friends on a sports team. You might find new friends in your neighbourhood.

▶Choose friends who enjoy doing the things you enjoy. These children share a love of basketball.

▲ If you enjoy science, find friends who also enjoy science.

Find friends who like the things you like. If you like drawing, look for friends who like to draw. If you like swimming or cycling, find friends who like these things, too.

▲ A smile tells everyone that you are friendly.

To make a friend, smile and say, "Hi." Look your new friend in the eyes and invite him or her to join you in a game or activity. Being kind shows that you will be a good friend.

Making friends can be scary, but you'll get better and better at it. If the first person you talk to doesn't want to be your friend, don't give up. There are lots of children who would like to have you for a friend.

▲Sharing something you enjoy is a good way to begin a friendship.

◄ Good friends like spending time together.

Treat your friends the way you would like to be treated. Good friends don't put pressure on each other. Good friends respect each other's **decisions**.

◄ Good friends cheer each other up.

Good friends are kind to each other. They tell the truth and keep their promises. Good friends stick up for each other.

Talk to an adult

You can make many **decisions** for yourself. But it's always good to talk to your parents about your decisions. Tell your parents if you are feeling peer pressure. They may have good ideas to help you solve the problem.

◄ Parents can help.

▲Play leaders can help.

Talk to your play leader, your club leader, or your grandparents. Your teacher and headteacher may be able to help, too. Adults know how hard it is to face peer pressure.

◄ Teachers can help.

Sometimes peers won't take "No" for an answer. If your peers treat you badly or scare you, tell an adult right away. If your peers make you feel unsafe, tell a parent, teacher, or other helpful adult.

▲School should be a safe
and happy place.

Adults need to know when there is a
problem so that they can help you.
Telling will help both you and your peers.
It may help other children, too. It can be
a brave thing to do.

Glossary

decision choice

encourage help and support

gossip unkind talk about other people

harmful may cause you to hurt yourself

peer person the same age or in the same class

peer pressure when peers get you to do things you don't want to do

respect think about the ideas and beliefs of others in a good way

Find out more

Books to read

Feelings: Caring, Sarah Medina (Raintree, 2007)

Feelings: Proud, Sarah Medina (Raintree, 2007)

Kids' Guides: Playground Survival, Kate Tym (Raintree, 2004)

Problem Solvers: Why Be Bossy? Janine Amos (Cherry Tree Books, 2003)

Websites

- ChildLine has a website (http://www.childline.org.uk) that gives information and advice on dealing with all sorts of problems that children may ask about.

- Kidscape (http://www.kidscape.org.uk/childrenteens/index.asp) is a group that works to stop bullying from happening.

Index

Pinch

OF

Nom

QUICK & EASY

First published 2020 by Bluebird
an imprint of Pan Macmillan
The Smithson, 6 Briset Street, London EC1M 5NR
EU representative: Macmillan Publishers Ireland Ltd, Mallard Lodge, Lansdowne Village, Dublin 4

Associated companies throughout the world
www.panmacmillan.com

ISBN 978-1-5290-3498-1

9

A CIP catalogue record for this book is available from the British Library.
Printed and bound in Great Britain by Bell & Bain Ltd, Glasgow

Publisher Carole Tonkinson
Managing Editor Martha Burley
Project Editor Laura Nickoll
Desk Editor Isabel Hewitt
Senior Production Controller Sarah Badhan
Art Direction and Design Nikki Dupin & Emma Wells, Nic&Lou
Illustration Shutterstock / Emma Wells
Food Styling Kate Wesson
Prop Styling Cynthia Blackett

Visit www.panmacmillan.com to read more about all our books
and to buy them. You will also find features, author interviews and
news of any author events, and you can sign up for e-newsletters
so that you're always first to hear about our new releases.

KATE ALLINSON & KAY FEATHERSTONE

Pinch

OF

Nom

QUICK & EASY

100 DELICIOUS,
SLIMMING RECIPES

bluebird
books for life

Contents

WELCOME to Pinch of Nom

QUICK & EASY!

HELLO

We can't quite believe we've made it to a third cookbook! We have been listening to all of your feedback and suggestions for this book and we're thrilled to be able to offer this set of recipes that are all quick and/or easy to make. Eighty of the recipes are brand new, with twenty being some of our most popular quick and easy website recipes. Now, more than ever, we know how important it is to prepare speedy and nutritious food using simple ingredients, so we really hope this book helps you to create some quick and easy, tasty grub.

SO WHY QUICK and EASY?

There are several reasons we decided to release a book for quick and easy recipes. Firstly, we have received overwhelming feedback from you all, suggesting that the meals you really need help with are the ones when you have little time or energy to create something healthy. We wanted to make it easy to still be mindful of your calorie intake, even when your motivation is low or you're short on time.

A FLEXIBLE WAY TO COOK

We wrote most of these recipes just before COVID-19 entirely changed our lives and we were conscious that we needed the recipes to work for whatever the landscape looked like in the future.

We needed simple ingredients with straightforward swaps for ingredients that were harder to get hold of.

You'll notice throughout the book we have noted ingredients that can be swapped easily in our SWAP THIS boxes – this will help at all times, but particularly in times where ingredients are hard to come by. You don't have to rigidly stick to the ingredients listed – if you have other veg that you want to use up, bung it into the dish. If you don't have one ingredient, try and swap it for something similar. These recipes are a blueprint, but feel free to make them your own and play around – there are no mistakes in cooking, just learning experiences!

Kate and Kay x

THE FOOD

As a classically trained chef, Kate has always looked at recipes and dishes and then worked on how to improve or recreate them. That is still the case and it's how the Pinch of Nom recipes are formed. Alongside her small team, the aim is to come up with the best ideas for recipes, then get into the kitchen and throw around ingredients until the right balance is made!

It is important to the Pinch of Nom team that all of the recipes are easily accessible and that they use ingredients that can be used time and again to save on cost. Ingredients that may seem less common are only ever featured where they add a unique touch to the dish and we have ensured that they pop up in many other deserving recipes.

We've also made sure that the recipes work for whatever cooking ability you have. We're confident that even the novice cook can tackle these recipes and end up with a decent meal without spending hours in the kitchen.

An impressive forty of the 100 recipes in this book are vegetarian. However, by being careful with types of ingredients used (vegetarian hard cheese, for example), or using a protein replacement of your choice, almost all the recipes can be made vegetarian, and many can be made vegan too. We've flagged vegetarian and vegan recipes, and we've added notes for when substitutions need to be made.

Recipe TAGS

EVERYDAY LIGHT

These recipes can be used freely throughout the week. All the meals, including accompaniments, are under 400 calories. Or, in the case of sides, snacks and sweet treats, under 200 calories. Of course, if you're counting calories, you still need to keep an eye on the values, but these recipes should help you stay under your allowance.

WEEKLY INDULGENCE

These recipes are still low in calories at between 400 and 500 calories, or 200–300 for sides, snacks and sweet treats, but should be saved for once or twice a week. Mix them into your Everyday Light recipes for variety.

SPECIAL OCCASION

These recipes are often lower in calories than their full-fat counterparts, but they need to be saved for a special occasion. This tag indicates any main meals that are over 500 calories or over 300 for sides, snacks and sweet treats.

KCALS *and* CARB VALUES

All of our recipes have been worked out as complete meals, using standardized portion sizes for any accompaniments as advised by the British Nutrition Foundation. Carb values are included for those who need to measure their intake.

GLUTEN-FREE RECIPES

We have marked gluten-free recipes with the icon as listed below. In all these recipes, we have assumed the use of gluten-free variants of common ingredients, such as stock cubes and Worcestershire sauce. Please check the labelling to ensure the product you buy is gluten-free.

SUPER QUICK *and* SUPER EASY

We've highlighted recipes that are either super quick, or super easy. If they are super quick, they are ready in 20 minutes or under. And if they are super easy, they have been highlighted because of a particularly simple method – perhaps the whole recipe is cooked in one pot, or it only features four ingredients. While all the recipes in this book are either quick, easy or both, we thought you'd appreciate a little pointer for those recipes that you can whip up after a long day and not feel like you've been in the kitchen all evening.

OUR RECIPE ICONS

V Suitable for vegetarians

VE Suitable for vegans

F Suitable for freezing
For all freezer-friendly recipes, we recommend defrosting completely before heating until piping hot.

GF Suitable for those following a gluten-free diet

All of these calculations and dietary indicators are for guidance only and are not to be taken as complete fact without checking ingredients and product labelling yourself.

BATCH COOKING

We've grouped our favourite batch-cooking recipes together in their own chapter, because batch-cooking ideas are often requested by our community and batch cooking often lends itself to being... quick and easy! As you can see, these recipes have their own specific guidelines, but there are also plenty of other recipes in the book that you can batch cook with a few tweaks, such as upping the portions of something like the Dirty Macaroni and freezing a batch for a later date. Some general notes to think about when batch cooking are below. It's always important to store food safely, so we have included the latest NHS food-safety guidelines (correct at the time of writing).

- **Divide the food into individual portions to refrigerate or freeze.** This means you can just reheat one portion, or four portions, or six etc., without needing to chisel portions off one big frozen block! It will also ensure they cool and freeze (and defrost) quicker.

- **Make sure you've got enough space** in your fridge or freezer for your meals before you get cooking!

- **Use refrigerated foods within 2 days.**

- **When freezing food**, make sure you use airtight containers or freezer bags that are suitable for the freezer. Invest in some decent, freezer- and microwave-proof storage containers. If not, your containers may crack or melt, which is not what you need when you want a quick meal you've spent time batch cooking. Make sure your containers are sealed properly to avoid 'freezer burn', which is when the food has been damaged by oxidation from air getting inside.

- **Always label food.** Use freezer-proof stickers to label your dish, adding the date when you made it. Nobody wants mystery food in the freezer, and it's likely it will end up going to waste. Meals can be frozen for 3–6 months. Up to 3 months is ideal and beyond 6 months is still safe, but the food may not taste as good.

- **Always make sure food is defrosted thoroughly**, either in the fridge or microwave, before reheating it.

- **Only reheat food once.**

- **When food has defrosted completely**, it should be reheated and eaten within 24 hours, so only defrost what you need. NHS guidelines state you should reheat food until it reaches 70°C/130°F and holds that temperature for 2 minutes. Make sure it is piping hot all the way through. Stir during reheating to ensure this.

- **You may freeze the sauce or meat for some recipes**, but need to cook rice, pasta or other accompaniments at the time you want to eat as they either cannot be reheated, or they're a lot nicer cooked fresh. Keep an eye out for the freezer instructions throughout the book for further details on each recipe.

- **If you are batch cooking rice**, it's important you store it correctly before you reheat it. You should cool it as quickly as possible, ideally within 1 hour. (With other foods this could be up to 2 hours.) You can put rice in a wide, shallow container, which will help it cool quicker due to the larger surface area. There is a risk of bacteria growing the longer it is left at room temperature. Cooked rice should only be kept in the fridge for 1 day before reheating. When you reheat rice, make sure it is piping hot all the way through. Never reheat rice more than once.

KEY INGREDIENTS

PROTEIN

Lean meats are a great source of protein, providing essential nutrients and fantastic filling power. In all cases where meat is used in this recipe book, you will need to ensure you are using the leanest cuts and trimming off all fats. Fish is another great source of protein and naturally low in fat. Pinch of Nom's favourite phrase? If it swims, it slims! Fish provides nutrients that the body struggles to produce naturally, making it perfect for some of Pinch of Nom's super slimming recipes. Vegetarian protein options can always be used instead of meat in all of the recipes in this book.

HERBS and SPICES

Pinch of Nom loves a bit of spice! One of the best ways to keep your food interesting when changing ingredients for lower fat/sugar/calorie versions is to season well with herbs and spices. In particular, mixed spice blends are perfect for certain recipes in this book. Don't be shy with spices – not all of them burn your mouth off!

STOCKS and SAUCES

When you remove fat from a dish, flavours can dwindle. Most people simply make something spicy to counteract the lack of flavours from fat, but sometimes the level of acidity in a dish is much more important. That's why we love vinegar, soy, fish sauce and Worcestershire sauce for boosting flavour and balancing out a dish. In addition, one of Pinch of Nom's most essential ingredients is the lowly stock pot. Stock pots add instant flavour and are so versatile. Pinch of Nom use various flavoured pots throughout this book, but they are all very interchangeable. It is worth noting that these stock pots and sauces are often high in salt, so swap for reduced-salt varieties if you prefer.

LEMONS and LIMES

Lemons and limes pack an absolute punch when it comes to flavour. They're perfect for adding to a dish, such as in the Lemon and Garlic Asparagus, where it just adds that extra bit of zing.

REDUCED-FAT DAIRY

Substituting some high-fat dairy products for some clever alternatives can make a dish instantly lower in calories. Quark and reduced-fat soft cheese or spreadable cheese are some essentials that Pinch of Nom are always looking to substitute for higher-fat versions.

TINS

Don't be afraid to bulk buy some of those tinned essentials! Beans, tomatoes, sweetcorn... You'll find many of these ingredients can be dumped into Pinch of Nom stews and salads. They keep the cost down and make little to no difference to the taste of these sorts of dishes in comparison with their fresh counterparts.

FROZEN FRUIT *and* VEG

Similarly, frozen fruit and vegetables make great filler ingredients and are great low-cost alternatives where fresh options aren't necessarily required, for stews etc. They usually have the added bonus of being pre-cut and pre-prepared, so it's the perfect time-saver for these quick and easy recipes!

PULSES, RICE *and* BEANS

High in both protein and fibre, keeping a few tins of beans and pulses in the cupboard is never going to harm! Rice is a fantastic filler and, flavoured with spices and/or seasoning, is a great accompaniment to many Pinch of Nom recipes.

BREAD

A great source of fibre and therefore providing that all-important filling power, wholemeal bread can be used as it is, or crumbed down to bind ingredients, such as in the Vegetable and Chickpea Roast. We often also use gluten-free breads, as they tend to contain fewer calories and less sugar, making them an easy swap to shave off some calories.

EGGS

Eggs are protein-rich, filling, tasty and versatile! The ultimate in slimming yet filling ingredients, the humble egg is so versatile that it can be used as an integral ingredient in recipes such as our chocolate pancakes, or for meals where they're the starring role such as the Crustless Quiche Lorraine. You'll always want a box in the house.

LOW-CALORIE SPRAY

One of the best ways to cut down on oils and fats being used to cook with is to use a low-calorie spray. There is little difference to the way that most ingredients are cooked, but it can make a huge difference to the calories consumed.

READY-MADE PASTRY

We have a few recipes using pastry in this book. There's no need to become a pastry chef overnight – just buy it ready-made! Not only can you usually find a light version with reduced calories, but ain't nobody got the time to be making filo pastry!

MINIMUM FUSS · Maximum FLAVOUR

ESSENTIAL KIT

NON-STICK PANS

If there's one bit of kit that Pinch of Nom would advise as investment kitchen pieces, it would be a decent set of non-stick pans. The better the non-stick quality of your pans, the less cooking oils and fats you will need to avoid food sticking to your pan and burning. Keep your pans in good health too – clean them properly and gently with soapy water. We recommend a good set of saucepans, a large frying pan and a griddle pan if you can – a few of our recipes call for a griddle pan, but you can use a frying pan if you can't get your hands on one.

FINE GRATER

Using a fine grater is one of those surprising revelations. You won't believe the difference in grating cheese with a fine grater versus a standard grater. 45g of cheese, for example, can easily cover an oven dish when using a fine grater. We also use the fine grater for citrus zest and for garlic and ginger. It helps a little go a long way.

KNIFE SHARPENER

There is nothing worse than trying to chop up a butternut squash with a spoon, so why would you recreate the experience with your knives? Keep those babies sharp! It will save you so much time and effort.

POTATO MASHER

Used in a variety of recipes, you'll need a decent masher to ensure you're not straining muscles every time you want a bit of mash!

FOOD PROCESSOR / BLENDER / STICK BLENDER

Essential pieces of kit for a lot of Pinch of Nom recipes. As quite a few of the recipes involve making sauces from scratch, a decent blender or food processor will be a godsend! A stick blender can also be used on most occasions if you're looking for something a bit cheaper or more compact. It's worth the cost of this equipment for all those flavourful and handmade sauces.

TUPPERWARE *and* PLASTIC TUBS

Most of the Pinch of Nom recipes in this book are freezable and ideal for batch cooking. Planning ahead is so much easier when you can cook ahead too. So invest in some decent freezer-proof tubs for storage.

OVENWARE

Used in a high percentage of Pinch of Nom dishes, oven trays and dishes are an essential bit of kit – keep them in good condition for longer by using disposable baking paper or foil to line them before cooking. We recommend some trays, a large heavy-based casserole dish with a lid and a lasagne dish as essentials.

SLOW COOKER

We are big fans of the slow cooker. Throw some ingredients in, go off and enjoy your day and return to a home-cooked meal, ready and waiting. They are also a relatively inexpensive bit of kit that will save you a lot of time. Quick and easy!

SET OF MEASURING SPOONS

Want to make sure you're not putting a tablespoon of chilli in your dish, rather than half a teaspoon? This is one of the most essential items of kitchenware you'll ever require. Especially, if you've ever made the aforementioned mistake, as Pinch of Nom has never done. Not ever.

ELECTRIC HAND WHISK

Have you ever tried to make meringue or whip cream with a hand whisk? I can still feel the arm throb! Of course, if working out while you cook is good for you, then just get a good old whisk. However, we would recommend using an electric whisk – they're relatively inexpensive and much less effort!

'Pinch of Nom has
shown me that even
a busy mum of two can
cook delicious, hearty,
healthy family meals...
and with all the amazing
recipes on Pinch of Nom
I've managed to lose
3 stone so far on my
weight-loss journey.'

KATIE

CHAPTER 1

BREAK
FAST

LOTUS BISCOFF AMERICAN PANCAKES

🕐 **8 MINS**   🍲 **10 MINS**   🍴 **SERVES 2**

PER SERVING:
307 KCAL /29G CARBS

40g instant oat cereal
100ml skimmed milk
2 medium eggs
2 tbsp Lotus Biscoff spread
2 tsp low-calorie caramel syrup
low-calorie cooking spray
1 Lotus Biscoff biscuit, crushed

There's no better way to start your morning than with these delicious, fluffy American-style pancakes! They're really easy and quick to make and require just a few basic ingredients to whip up. Flavoured with Lotus Biscoff spread and topped with crunchy biscuits, these pancakes may taste really naughty but they're actually low on calories and slimming friendly!

Everyday Light ───────────────

Add the instant oat cereal, milk and eggs to a bowl and whisk until combined. Add 1 tbsp of Lotus Biscoff spread and the caramel syrup and mix again. Leave to rest for 5 minutes.

Spray a frying pan with low-calorie cooking spray and place over a medium heat. When the pan is hot, spoon 2 tbsp of mixture into the pan and spread into little pancake shapes. Don't spread the mixture out too far as you want them to be nice and fluffy. It's best to cook two pancakes at once, if your pan is big enough.

Cook the first side for 2 minutes until little bubbles appear on the surface, then flip over to cook the other side. The pancakes should be a golden colour.

Once the first batch is cooked, stack them on a plate and cover in foil to keep them warm. Move onto the next batch until all of the mixture is used up.

Spread a little of the rest of the Lotus Biscoff spread onto each pancake. Stack them up and top with the crushed biscuit.

SWAP THIS: You can use rolled oats instead of instant oats, you will just need to blitz them into a fine powder using a food processor first.

TIP: You can cook two or more pancakes at once depending on the size of the frying pan – just make sure to leave enough room to spread the mixture into the pancake shapes.

BANANA DIPPERS

🕐 **5 MINS**   🍲 **6 MINS**   ✕ **SERVES 2**

PER SERVING:
318 KCAL / 49G CARBS

FOR THE DIPPERS
50g plain flour
50ml skimmed milk
½ tsp vanilla extract
1 medium egg
low-calorie cooking spray
2 bananas
1 tsp icing sugar

FOR THE SAUCE
30g quark
1 tbsp chocolate spread
1 tsp sugar-free chocolate syrup

Soft bananas coated in a crispy pancake batter and served with a chocolate dipping sauce? It doesn't get much better than that! These Banana Dippers are delicious when served either for breakfast or as an afternoon snack. The slimming-friendly chocolate sauce feels super indulgent and we think that some sliced strawberries finish this dish off perfectly!

Everyday Light ————————————————

To make the batter, put the flour, milk, vanilla extract and egg in a mixing bowl and whisk until smooth. Set aside to rest.

In a separate bowl mix the quark, chocolate spread and chocolate syrup until combined. Set aside until ready to serve.

Spray a frying pan with low-calorie cooking spray and place over a medium heat. Slice the bananas in half and then each half lengthways into three sections. Dip each banana slice into the batter mixture until coated, then place into the hot frying pan. Cook each dipper for 2–3 minutes on each side, until golden brown in colour and a little crispy round the edges.

Put the dippers onto a plate and dust with icing sugar. Serve with the dipping sauce and enjoy.

TIP: Use tongs to dip the banana in the batter mixture. Make sure you use nice, ripe bananas for a soft centre in the dippers.

JAMMY DODGER FRENCH TOAST

⏱ **10 MINS** 🍲 **15 MINS** ✕ **SERVES 2**

PER SERVING:

273 KCAL / 35G CARBS

4 slices wholemeal bread,
  approximately 30g per slice
3 tbsp reduced-sugar strawberry jam
2 eggs, beaten with a fork
10ml semi-skimmed milk
2 tbsp granulated sweetener
2 tsp ground cinnamon
low-calorie cooking spray
1 tsp icing sugar

TO ACCOMPANY *(optional)*
4 tbsp fat-free Greek
  yoghurt sweetened with
  ½–1 tsp granulated sweetener
  and 4 sliced strawberries (about
  30g each) (+ 78 kcal per serving)

Adorable heart-shaped French toast with a fruity jam filling, dusted with sweet cinnamon. Perfect for that special someone – if you can bear to hand it over, that is!

Everyday Light

Preheat the oven to 200°C (fan 180°C/gas mark 6).

Using a 12cm (4in)-wide heart-shaped cutter, cut all the pieces of bread into heart shapes. Using a 5cm (2in) circle cutter, cut out a circle on two of the slices of bread. Discard the excess bread.

Spread half of the jam on the two plain, heart-shaped slices of bread, then place the slices with the circles cut out on top.

In a deep dish add the beaten egg and milk along with 1 tbsp of the granulated sweetener and 1 tsp of the cinnamon. Mix well. Carefully dip the bread into the egg mix, coating both sides.

Spray a frying pan with low-calorie cooking spray and fry the bread for 5 minutes on both sides until golden brown. Place the bread on a baking tray with the circle side face up, add the remaining jam to the circle and put into the oven for 10 minutes.

In a small bowl mix the remaining cinnamon and granulated sweetener together and sprinkle over the cooked toast. Serve with a light dusting of icing sugar.

SWAP THIS: Use any other flavour of jam instead of the strawberry jam.

TIP: Put excess bread into the freezer to use later for breadcrumbs.

BUBBLE *and* SQUEAK

🕐 **15 MINS**   🍲 **55 MINS**   ✕ **SERVES 4**

PER SERVING:
203 KCAL / 32G CARBS

4 medium potatoes, about
   150g each, peeled and cut
   into large chunks
150g Savoy cabbage, roughly
   shredded into 5mm (¼in)-wide
   strips
low-calorie cooking spray
1 onion, peeled and thinly sliced
1 garlic clove, peeled and crushed
4 smoked bacon medallions, cut
   into 2cm (¾in) squares
sea salt and freshly ground
   black pepper

TO ACCOMPANY *(optional)*
poached egg (+ 74 kcal per
   serving)

Traditionally, Bubble and Squeak is made with potatoes and cabbage, but you could also add any other vegetables that you might have hanging around, like peas or carrots. This classic British dish can be made from scratch with fresh ingredients, but it's also the perfect way to use up leftover veg from your Sunday roast. Serve with a poached egg on top for a really hearty, delicious breakfast!

Everyday Light

Place the potato chunks in a pan of boiling water, cover and reduce the heat to simmer for 20–25 minutes. When done, the potatoes should be soft when tested with a knife. Drain the potatoes and mash well. Set aside.

Place the cabbage in a pan of boiling water, cover and simmer for 3–4 minutes. Drain the cabbage well and add to the pan that contains the mashed potato. Mix thoroughly.

Spray a medium frying pan with low-calorie cooking spray and place over a medium heat. Add the onion and fry for 5–10 minutes, stirring, until softened and golden brown. Add the garlic and bacon to the onion and fry for a further 5 minutes, stirring. Add the onion, garlic and bacon to the pan of potato and cabbage. Season well with salt and pepper. Mix until completely combined.

Spray a little low-calorie cooking spray into the frying pan and place over a high heat. Tip in the mixture and form into a large patty or into eight small patties, if preferred. Fry for 10 minutes on each side, or until brown and crispy and hot right through.

SWAP THIS: Use any leftover cooked veg such as peas, carrots and sprouts instead of the cabbage.

TIP: Make sure you drain the cabbage really well, otherwise it will make the potato mixture too wet.

DILL CREAM CHEESE *and* SMOKED SALMON BAGEL

🕐 **2 MINS**   🍲 **NO COOK**   ✕ **SERVES 1**

PER SERVING:
231 KCAL / 27G CARBS

1 wholemeal bagel thin
40g reduced-fat cream cheese
2 sprigs fresh dill, leaves only,
   finely chopped, plus extra to
   serve (optional)
½ tsp lemon juice
freshly ground black pepper
20g smoked salmon

TO ACCOMPANY *(optional)*
35g thinly sliced cucumber
   (+ 6 kcal) and some fresh dill

Super quick and really easy, this recipe is perfect for breakfast, brunch or lunch! It's a simple meal for any day of the week, but we think it's an especially good choice for breakfast on Christmas morning or at the weekend. We've used smoked salmon on our bagel, but, if you'd prefer, you could keep the cost low by using smoked salmon trimmings instead!

Everyday Light

If you want your bagel toasted pop it in the toaster until lightly browned.

While the bagel is toasting, mix the reduced-fat cream cheese, dill, lemon juice and pepper in a small bowl. Spread the cream cheese onto the bagel and lay the smoked salmon on top. You can add some optional thinly sliced cucumber and more fresh dill to serve if you like!

SWAP THIS: Use half a standard bagel or wholemeal toast instead of the wholemeal bagel thin or swap the fresh dill for fresh chives.

'Pinch of Nom takes the stress out of cooking! The meals are delicious and filling and I feel proud of what I've been able to cook, particularly when it's so tasty!'

TORI

BREAKFAST POTATOES

🕐 **10 MINS**   🍲 **40 MINS**   ✕ **SERVES 4**

use veggie
Worcestershire sauce

VE F GF

use Henderson's
relish

PER SERVING:
200 KCAL / 40G CARBS

600g potatoes, with skin left on,
  washed and cut into
  2cm (¾in) cubes
3 mixed peppers, halved,
  deseeded and thinly sliced
2 onions, peeled and thinly sliced
low-calorie cooking spray
1 tsp Worcestershire sauce
1 tsp onion granules
½ tsp smoked paprika
¼ tsp garlic granules
sea salt and freshly ground
  black pepper
2 spring onions, trimmed
  and sliced

TO ACCOMPANY *(optional)*
egg fried in low-calorie cooking
  spray (+ 101 kcal per serving)
  or ¼ sliced avocado
  (+ 69 kcal per serving)

These American-style Breakfast Potatoes are usually cooked in oil, but we've kept them healthier by using a low-calorie cooking spray instead. They're a great choice when you need a filling breakfast that doesn't involve bread, and are delicious served with a fried egg, a quarter of an avocado or on the side of your healthy fry-up. This recipe also works really well with sweet potatoes, if you fancy a bit of a change!

Everyday Light ———————————————

Add the diced potatoes to a medium saucepan of cold water. Bring to the boil then reduce the heat to a simmer for 7 minutes. When ready, the potatoes should still be firm but starting to become tender.

While the potatoes are cooking, place the peppers and onions in a large frying pan which has been coated in low-calorie cooking spray. Cook over a medium heat for 15 minutes until softened.

Drain the potatoes and add them to the frying pan with the onions and peppers. Stir in the Worcestershire sauce, onion granules, paprika and garlic granules. Spray with some more low-calorie cooking spray and season well with salt and pepper. Cook for another 10–15 minutes over a medium heat, or until the potatoes are cooked through but still hold their shape.

Serve with a fried egg or a quarter of an avocado for a slimming but filling breakfast, scattered with spring onions. You can also cool and freeze any leftover potatoes.

SWAP THIS: Swap the potatoes for sweet potatoes (they may need less cooking time, as they tend to cook faster), or the peppers for mushrooms.

SQUASHAGE FINGERS

Super QUICK

🕐 **10 MINS**   🍲 **10 MINS**   ✕ **SERVES 4**

F **GF** *use GF Worcestershire sauce or Henderson's relish* ↱

PER SERVING:
344 KCAL /23G CARBS

FOR THE SQUASHAGE FINGERS
400g 5%-fat pork mince
¼ tsp dried parsley
¼ tsp garlic granules
¼ tsp mustard powder
½ tsp Worcestershire sauce
low-calorie cooking spray
sea salt and freshly ground
  black pepper

FOR THE ROLLS
4 smoked bacon medallions, cut
  into strips
4 gluten-free finger rolls or
  wholemeal hotdog buns, 60g each
40g reduced-fat Cheddar, grated

FOR THE QUICK KETCHUP
4 tbsp tomato puree
1 tsp Worcestershire sauce
1 tsp white wine vinegar
pinch of paprika
pinch of granulated sweetener
sea salt and freshly ground
  black pepper

We've crossed a breakfast patty with sausages that are a little squashed, and come up with squashages! We've topped them with bacon and ketchup in a bun to make a breakfast hotdog (there are no hard-and-fast breakfast rules here!) but they also work well in place of traditional sausages in a classic cooked breakfast.

Everyday Light

Mix all the squashage finger ingredients together, apart from the low-calorie cooking spray. Split the squashage mix into four. With your hands roll into four long, finger-length sausage shapes.

Spray a large frying pan with low-calorie cooking spray. Lay the sausages in the pan and squish them down gently so they don't roll about. They will be about the thickness of a burger.

Add the bacon strips to the same pan as the squashage fingers. Cook over a medium heat for about 10 minutes (flipping the fingers halfway through) until the squashages are cooked through and the bacon is browned. If you're not sure whether the squashages are completely cooked through, you can cut into the top of one with a knife to check.

While the squashages and bacon are cooking, mix together the quick ketchup ingredients in a bowl – you can use shop-bought ketchup if you prefer!

When the squashages are ready, add one to each bun with a sprinkle of cheese, some of the ketchup and some of the bacon strips. You can serve them like this or place under a hot grill for a few minutes to melt the cheese if you prefer.

You can freeze any cooked, leftover squashages for another day, or if you want to plan ahead then you can also freeze the raw mixture!

SWAP THIS: Swap the pork mince for turkey or beef mince.

CHOCOLATE BANANA MUFFINS

⏱ **10 MINS**   🍲 **25 MINS**   ✕ **SERVES 12**

PER SERVING:
149 KCAL / 26G CARBS

3 medium, ripe bananas, peeled
    and mashed (about 320g total,
    mashed weight)
2 large eggs, beaten with a fork
125ml maple syrup
1 tsp vanilla extract
225g plain wholemeal flour
25g cocoa powder
1 tsp baking powder
25g plain chocolate chips

These delicious muffins taste so indulgent that you'd never believe they were slimming friendly! Made with wholemeal flour to help keep you feeling full until lunchtime, and sweetened using only maple syrup and ripe bananas, these tasty treats contain no fat and are super low on calories. Great for a quick breakfast on the go, or an afternoon treat alongside a cup of tea or coffee.

Everyday Light

Preheat the oven to 200°C (fan 180°C/gas mark 6). Place twelve paper muffin cases in a 12-hole muffin tin.

Put the mashed bananas, egg, maple syrup and vanilla extract in a large bowl and mix well with a wooden spoon. Sift the flour, cocoa powder and baking powder into the banana mixture and then tip in anything left in the sieve. Mix well with a wooden spoon until completely combined.

Divide the mixture between the twelve muffin cases and place the chocolate chips on the top of each muffin. Place in the preheated oven and bake for 20–25 minutes. To check that the muffins are done, insert a sharp knife into the centre. It should come out clean when they're ready. Transfer the muffins to a cooling rack to cool.

Fakeaways

CHAPTER 2

THAI BASIL CHICKEN

🕐 **5 MINS**   🍲 **15 MINS**   ✕ **SERVES 4**

PER SERVING:
240 KCAL / 17G CARBS

low-calorie cooking spray
2 onions, peeled and chopped
2 fresh chillies, finely diced (leave
   the seeds in if you like extra spice)
4 garlic cloves, peeled and minced
500g skinless chicken breast,
   finely chopped
2 medium peppers, deseeded
   and diced
3 tbsp oyster sauce
2 tbsp soy sauce
2 tsp fish sauce
2 tsp granulated sweetener
   (adjust to taste)
250g frozen green beans
60g fresh basil, thick stalks
   removed and roughly torn
50g fresh spinach, roughly torn

TO ACCOMPANY *(optional)*
80g steamed vegetables (+ 38 kcal
   per serving) or 50g uncooked
   basmati rice per portion, cooked
   according to packet instructions
   (+ 173 kcal per 125g cooked
   serving)

This quick recipe is our British take on a popular street food dish from Thailand. Traditionally this dish would be made with Thai holy basil, which has a more peppery taste than other varieties, however it still works really well with the standard basil you can pick up in the supermarket. Use whichever you can get hold of!

Weekly Indulgence

Spray a large frying pan or wok with low-calorie cooking spray. Place over a medium heat, add the onions, chillies and garlic and fry for 5 minutes to release the aromatics and soften the onions slightly. Add the chicken and peppers to the pan with the oyster sauce, soy sauce, fish sauce and sweetener. Fry for 5 minutes over a medium heat until the chicken has cooked through. Add the frozen green beans to the pan and fry for a further 5 minutes until they are cooked through.

Remove from the heat and stir through the basil and spinach until it wilts. Serve with an accompaniment of your choice. (You can also cool and freeze for another day.)

SWAP THIS: Swap the chopped chicken for turkey mince or chopped pork steak, or use skinless, boneless chicken thigh instead of breast meat.

CHAR SIU PORK BURGERS

🕐 20 MINS   🍲 7 MINS   ✕ SERVES 4

F

PER SERVING:
319 KCAL / 25G CARBS

FOR THE BURGERS
1 small courgette, coarsely grated
500g 5%-fat pork mince
2 spring onions, trimmed and
  thinly sliced
low-calorie cooking spray

FOR THE CHAR SIU GLAZE
6 tbsp oyster sauce
2 tsp grated root ginger
2 garlic cloves, peeled and crushed
1 tsp Chinese 5-spice
1 tsp rice vinegar
1 tsp granulated sweetener

FOR THE SLAW
2 pak choi, washed and sliced
1 medium carrot, peeled and
  grated or cut into thin strips
  (julienne)
2 spring onions, trimmed and
  thinly sliced
2 tbsp rice vinegar
1 tsp light soy sauce
1 tsp granulated sweetener
4 wholemeal bread rolls

These burgers are inspired by char siu, which is a Cantonese barbecue pork dish and a popular flavour in Chinese cuisine. We've used 5%-fat pork mince to keep the calories low and have added some extra veggies into the burgers in order to keep them nice and moist. A fresh, Asian-style slaw complements the flavours of the burgers perfectly and means they're great when served at a summer barbecue!

Everyday Light ─────────────────────

Wrap the grated courgette in a clean tea towel and squeeze out the excess liquid. You may be surprised at how much comes out! Place the courgette in a large bowl, along with the pork mince and the sliced spring onion. Mix well, then shape into four burgers, either by hand or with a burger press. Place in the fridge while you make the slaw and the glaze (or you can freeze the burgers to make this dish another day).

Mix all the glaze ingredients together in a small bowl. Place the sliced pak choi, carrot and spring onion into a large bowl. Mix together the rice vinegar, light soy sauce and sweetener in a small bowl, pour over the slaw mix and toss lightly.

Now, cook your burgers. Place a griddle pan over a medium to high heat and spray with low-calorie cooking spray. Brush one side of the burgers liberally with the glaze and place in the griddle pan, glaze side down. Brush the top side with glaze, and after 2 minutes of cooking, carefully flip the burgers. Brush another layer of glaze on top, and after 2 more minutes, carefully flip again. Cook for 1 minute, while brushing the burgers with a final layer of glaze. Flip again and cook for a final minute or 2, or until the juices run clear.

Slice the bread rolls and fill with slaw. Place a burger in each and serve with any remaining slaw on the side.

SWAP THIS:
Swap pork mince
for turkey mince.

TERIYAKI CHICKEN

⏱ **15 MINS** 🍲 **40 MINS** ✕ **SERVES 4**

F **GF** *use GF soy sauce*

PER SERVING:
311 KCAL / 32G CARBS

3 tbsp dark soy sauce

2 tbsp rice wine vinegar

160ml fresh orange juice

2cm (¾in) piece of root ginger, peeled and finely chopped

4 garlic cloves, 2 peeled and chopped, 2 peeled and crushed

3 tbsp runny honey

4 skinless chicken breasts, about 140g each

2 peppers, deseeded and cut into chunks

2 carrots, peeled and cut into 2cm (¾in) chunks

2 red onions, peeled and cut in quarters

1 courgette, washed and cut into 2cm (¾in) chunks

1 tsp Chinese 5-spice

sea salt and freshly ground black pepper (1 tsp of each)

low-calorie cooking spray

2 spring onions, trimmed and chopped

TO ACCOMPANY *(optional)*
50g uncooked basmati rice per portion, cooked according to packet instructions (+ 173 kcal per 125g cooked serving)

SWAP THIS: Use chicken thighs instead of chicken breast, or use sliced chicken and stir-fry it before adding the vegetables and sauce.

This is our take on a classic, popular Japanese dish: tender chicken in a rich teriyaki sauce, served on a bed of fragrant roasted vegetables. Great for a Friday night fakeaway!

Weekly Indulgence ─────────────────────

Preheat the oven to 220°C (fan 200°C/gas mark 7).

In a large bowl mix the soy sauce, rice wine vinegar, orange juice, ginger, chopped garlic and honey. Add the chicken and coat well, then leave to one side.

Place the peppers, carrots, red onions, crushed garlic and courgette on a baking tray, season with Chinese 5-spice, salt and pepper and spray with low-calorie cooking spray. Cook in the oven for 40–45 minutes until the vegetables are tender, remembering to turn them twice during cooking.

While the vegetables are cooking, spray a medium frying pan with low-calorie cooking spray and place on a medium heat. Remove the chicken from the sauce, keeping the sauce for later. Fry the chicken in the frying pan for 2 minutes on both sides, until completely sealed. Place the chicken in an ovenproof dish and pour over the remainder of the sauce. Cover with foil and place in the oven. Cook for 20 minutes then remove the foil.

Cook for another 10–15 minutes uncovered until the chicken is cooked through with no traces of pink, and the sauce has thickened. Remove from the oven and serve the chicken on top of the vegetables with the sauce poured over. Sprinkle with the chopped spring onions.

TEX-MEX MEATBALLS

🕐 **10 MINS**　　🍲 **25 MINS**　　✕ **SERVES 4**

use Henderson's relish and GF stock cube ↘

F　**GF**

PER SERVING:
383 KCAL / 31G CARBS

FOR THE MEATBALLS
500g 2%-fat turkey mince
1 x 400g tin kidney beans, rinsed
　and crushed
1 x 260g tin sweetcorn, drained
1 egg
1 tsp garlic granules
1 tsp onion granules
½ tsp ground coriander
½ tsp paprika
½ tsp chilli powder
sea salt and freshly ground
　black pepper
low-calorie cooking spray

FOR THE SAUCE
1 onion, peeled and thinly sliced
1 medium pepper, deseeded and
　thinly sliced
low-calorie cooking spray
2 x 400g tins chopped tomatoes
1 tsp Worcestershire sauce
1 chicken stock cube, crumbled
1 tsp garlic granules
1 tsp paprika
pinch of chilli powder (adjust to taste)
sea salt and freshly ground
　black pepper
pinch of coriander leaves, to serve

TO ACCOMPANY *(optional)*
50g uncooked basmati rice per
　portion, cooked according to
　packet instructions (+ 173 kcal
　per 125g cooked serving) or 50g
　uncooked pasta per portion, cooked
　according to packet instructions
　(+ 174 kcal per 100g cooked serving)

These meatballs are a Tex-Mex twist on an Italian classic. To keep them light, we've used 2%-fat turkey mince, but you could also try 5%-fat pork or beef mince instead if you prefer a more traditional meatball; they taste just as good!

Weekly Indulgence ─────────

Preheat the oven to 220°C (fan 200°C/gas mark 7).

Mix the meatball ingredients together in a bowl. Shape into large meatballs. The mix should make about twenty meatballs slightly larger than a golf ball.

Line a baking tray with foil and spray with low-calorie cooking spray. Lay out the meatballs so that they're not touching and place in the middle of the oven for 25 minutes, until the turkey is white and cooked throughout.

While the meatballs are in the oven add the onion and pepper to the pan and gently fry in low-calorie cooking spray for 10 minutes until softened. Add the rest of the sauce ingredients and stir. Reduce the heat to low and simmer for 15 minutes until the meatballs are ready. Add the meatballs to the sauce and serve with an accompaniment of your choice, sprinkled with the coriander leaves. You can also cool and pop them in the freezer to have another day.

SWAP THIS: Swap the turkey mince for beef or pork mince, or the kidney beans for other tinned beans (e.g. butter beans) or dried beans (soaked and cooked).

PORK LARB LETTUCE WRAPS

🕐 **5 MINS**   🍲 **10 MINS**   ✕ **SERVES 4**

PER SERVING:
189 KCAL / 2.9G CARBS

2 little gem lettuces
2½ tbsp fish sauce
juice of 1½ limes
½ tsp granulated sweetener
low-calorie cooking spray
3 garlic cloves, peeled
  and crushed
2 red chillies, deseeded – one
  finely chopped, the other
  thinly sliced
500g 5%-fat pork mince
4 spring onions, trimmed
  and sliced
handful of fresh mint,
  roughly chopped
handful of fresh Thai basil,
  roughly chopped
handful of fresh coriander,
  roughly chopped

A popular Thai street food, this pork larb is packed full of simply stunning Thai flavours. Tangy lime and savoury umami fish sauce with fresh herbs and a little chilli kick, wrapped in crispy fresh lettuce. Add a pinch of chilli flakes if you like it very spicy!

Everyday Light ————————————————

Break off all the leaves of the gem lettuces and give them a good wash under cold water and shake dry. Place in a serving bowl.

In a small bowl mix together the fish sauce, lime juice and sweetener to make a dressing.

Spray a wok or a large frying pan with low-calorie cooking spray and stir-fry the garlic and finely chopped chilli (save the sliced chilli for garnish later) over a medium heat for 1 minute. Increase to a high heat and add the pork mince to the wok. Stir-fry for 5 minutes, until the meat is opaque. Pour in two thirds of the dressing and continue to cook for another 2–3 minutes until the liquid has evaporated.

Allow to cool, then stir through the remaining dressing, spring onions and herbs. Place in a serving bowl and sprinkle with the sliced chilli. Serve with the bowl of lettuce and serving spoons, so people can pile the larb into the leaves and build their own wraps.

SWAP THIS:
Swap the pork mince for turkey mince.

TIP: If you want to be traditional, serve this with some toasted rice as a side to sprinkle on top. Toast 2 tbsp of raw basmati rice (+ 24 kcal per serving) in a dry non-stick frying pan for about 10 minutes until golden, then grind in a pestle and mortar or a food processor.

CHICKEN *and* BANANA CURRY

🕐 **10 MINS**   🍲 **40 MINS**   ✕ **SERVES 4**

F **GF**  *use GF stock cube*

PER SERVING:
346 KCAL / 24G CARBS

1 onion, peeled and quartered

3 garlic cloves, peeled

1 red chilli, deseeded

5cm (2in) piece of root ginger, peeled

low-calorie cooking spray

1 tbsp garam masala

50g ground almonds

500ml chicken stock (1 chicken stock cube, dissolved in 500ml boiling water)

500g chicken breasts (skin and visible fat removed), cut into chunks

2 tsp cornflour

140g fat-free Greek yoghurt

3 bananas, peeled and sliced

sea salt and freshly ground black pepper

4g fresh coriander, chopped

TO ACCOMPANY *(optional)*

50g uncooked basmati rice per portion, cooked according to packet instructions (+ 173 kcal per 125g cooked serving)

Ever heard the saying, 'Don't knock it until you've tried it'? If you've never tried banana in a savoury dish, you are in for a real treat! A takeaway favourite of ours, this curry contains similar flavours to a korma or Kashmiri dish. It's packed with tender chicken in a rich and creamy sauce, with added fibre and nutrition from the sliced bananas.

Special Occasion

Place the onion, garlic, chilli and ginger in a food processor and blend to a paste. Alternatively, chop very finely.

Spray a large frying pan with low-calorie cooking spray and place over a medium heat. Add the paste and fry for 10 minutes, stirring to avoid sticking. Add the garam masala, ground almonds and chicken stock and mix. Add the chicken and simmer for 25 minutes, or until the chicken is cooked right through. Mix the cornflour with the yoghurt and add to the frying pan. Simmer for 2 minutes until it starts to thicken, stirring well. Add the banana and cook for a further 2 minutes to heat through.

Season with salt and pepper to taste. Sprinkle with the chopped coriander and serve. The curry can also be frozen once cooled (make sure the dish is defrosted completely before reheating).

SWAP THIS: Swap the chicken breast for chicken thighs, or try fat-free natural yoghurt instead of fat-free Greek yoghurt.

BAKED CHIMICHANGA

🕐 **15 MINS**　🍲 **25 MINS**　✕ **SERVES 4**

GF *use GF wraps and Henderson's relish*

PER SERVING:
405 KCAL / 45G CARBS

FOR THE CHIMICHANGA
low-calorie cooking spray
1 small onion, peeled and sliced
½ red pepper, deseeded
　and sliced
1 tsp chilli powder (mild or hot
　depending on your preference)
½ tsp ground cumin
1½ tsp garlic granules
1 x 400g tin chopped tomatoes,
　drained
2 tsp Henderson's relish (or
　Worcestershire sauce)
juice of 1 lime
200g cooked chicken, shredded
1 x 400g tin black beans, drained
　and rinsed
4 low-calorie wraps
80g reduced-fat Cheddar, grated

FOR THE PICO DE GALLO
2 salad tomatoes, deseeded
　and cut into small dice
¼ red onion, peeled and finely
　chopped
10g fresh coriander, chopped
juice of ½ lime
pinch of dried chilli flakes
pinch of granulated sweetener
50g fat-free Greek yoghurt,
　to serve

TO ACCOMPANY *(optional)*
75g mixed salad (+ 15 kcal
　per serving)

Essentially a deep-fried burrito, a chimichanga is a Tex-Mex classic and is such an indulgent treat! A great way to use up leftover chicken, we've baked this dish in the oven to keep it slimming friendly without compromising on the delicious flavours. Serve with the refreshing pico de gallo and a dollop of Greek yoghurt – delish!

Weekly Indulgence

Place all of the ingredients for the pico de gallo in a small bowl and mix. Cover and refrigerate until needed. Preheat the oven to 200°C (fan 180°C/gas mark 6) and spray a baking sheet with low-calorie cooking spray.

Spray a large frying pan with low-calorie cooking spray and place over a medium heat. Add the onion and pepper and sauté for 3–4 minutes, until they're beginning to soften. Add the chilli powder, cumin and 1 tsp of the garlic granules. Cook for 1 minute until fragrant, then add the tomatoes, Henderson's relish and half the lime juice. Stir in the chicken and allow to heat through.

While the filling is heating through, mash the beans with the remaining ½ tsp of garlic granules and the other half of the lime juice.

Now assemble your wraps. Spread some bean mash over each wrap. Place a quarter of the filling towards the bottom of one wrap and sprinkle on a quarter of the cheese. Fold up the end, then fold in the two sides and roll up, keeping the edge sealed. Place the wrap on the prepared baking sheet then repeat with the other wraps.

Spray with low-calorie cooking spray and bake in the oven for 15–20 minutes until the wraps are crisp and golden. Serve topped with the pico de gallo and a spoon of Greek yoghurt.

CREAMY LENTIL DHAL

🕐 **15 MINS**   🍲 **30 MINS**   ✗ **SERVES 6**

use GF stock cubes ↗

(VE) (F) (GF)

PER SERVING:
208 KCAL / 31G CARBS

low-calorie cooking spray
1 large onion, peeled and
   finely chopped
3 garlic cloves, peeled
   and crushed
1 thumb-sized piece of root
   ginger, peeled and grated
2 tsp garam masala
1 tsp ground coriander
½ tsp ground cinnamon
1 x 400g tin chopped tomatoes
400ml dairy-free coconut milk
   alternative
150ml vegetable stock
   (2 vegetable stock cubes
   dissolved in 150ml boiling water)
1 carrot, peeled and grated
250g red lentils
juice of 1 lemon
50g baby spinach
a handful of coriander, chopped

TO ACCOMPANY *(optional)*
wholemeal roti
   (+ 166 kcal per serving, for
   a 58g roti)

Lentils are one of our favourite ingredients. High in fibre and protein, low in fat and, most importantly, tasty! Dhal is a classic dish that makes the most of these versatile pulses, and can easily be made gluten free and vegan too. We have swapped calorie-laden coconut milk for a dairy-free milk alternative. You still get the great coconut taste and creaminess, but with fewer calories!

Everyday Light ————————————————

Spray a saucepan with low-calorie cooking spray, place over a medium heat, add the onion and sauté for 5 minutes, until softened.

Add the garlic, ginger and spices and continue to cook for 1 minute to allow the spices to become fragrant. Pour in the tomatoes, coconut milk alternative and stock and stir well. Stir in the grated carrot and lentils. Bring to the boil, stir and cover, then turn down the heat and simmer for 20 minutes, stirring occasionally. The lentils should be tender but still holding their shape. Add the lemon juice then stir in the spinach and coriander. Continue stirring over the heat until the spinach has wilted. You can also cool and freeze for another day.

Serve as a side dish or with rice as a main meal.

'Pinch of Nom gives me the motivation to try meals out of my comfort zone. I never thought I would like trying new things... but I LOVE IT!'

REBECCA

VEGGIE SATAY NOODLES

🕐 **10 MINS**   🍲 **10 MINS**   ✕ **SERVES 4**

(V) (F)

PER SERVING:
308 KCAL / 46G CARBS

3 x 50g nests of egg noodles
low-calorie cooking spray
1 onion, peeled and thinly sliced
2cm (¾in) piece of root ginger,
   peeled and grated
3 garlic cloves, peeled and grated
½ red chilli, deseeded and chopped
1 red pepper, deseeded and
   thinly sliced
160g beansprouts
1 large carrot, peeled and
   thinly sliced
2 pak choi, sliced
½ tsp chilli powder
½ tsp garam masala
1 tsp ground turmeric
½ tsp ground cumin
2 tbsp soy sauce
1 tbsp vegetarian fish sauce
4 tbsp peanut butter powder
2 tsp cornflour
200ml dairy-free coconut milk
   alternative
juice of 1 lime
10g fresh coriander, chopped
pinch of dried chilli flakes

A traditional Thai dish full of crisp, fresh vegetables and coconut. The noodles are coated in a spicy peanut sauce using peanut butter powder and a dairy-free coconut milk alternative instead of coconut milk. This helps to keep all the fragrance and flavour for a fraction of the calories, while still satisfying the cravings for that satay taste!

Everyday Light

Cook the egg noodles in a pan of boiling salted water for 4 minutes then drain and rinse in cold water to stop any further cooking.

While the noodles are cooking, spray a wok or large frying pan with low-calorie cooking spray and fry the onion, ginger, garlic and fresh chilli over a medium heat for 2–3 minutes until soft. Add the red pepper, beansprouts, carrot and pak choi and cook for 2–3 minutes more.

In a mixing bowl, add chilli powder, garam masala, turmeric, cumin, soy sauce, fish sauce and mix together. Add the peanut butter powder to the bowl along with the cornflour, coconut milk alternative and lime juice and mix well.

Add the noodles to the vegetables and stir until combined.

Pour over the sauce, making sure to stir thoroughly until the vegetables and noodles are coated, and cook for a further 2–3 minutes to thicken the sauce. (Once the vegetables and noodles are ready, at this point you could let them cool, then freeze to have another day.)

Serve sprinkled with the chopped coriander and chilli flakes.

SWAP THIS: Use shredded cabbage or lettuce instead of pak choi, or butternut squash or carrot spaghetti or courgetti instead of noodles.

TIP: To add a lovely flavour and extra texture to this recipe you can add some chopped peanuts to garnish.

CREAMY VEGETABLE PANANG CURRY

🕐 **15 MINS**   🍲 **35 MINS**   ✕ **SERVES 4**

F **GF** *use GF stock cube*

PER SERVING:
264 KCAL / 23G CARBS

low-calorie cooking spray
400g tofu, cut into 2.5cm
   (1in) cubes
2 onions, peeled and sliced
2 medium carrots, peeled
   and thinly sliced
1 red pepper, deseeded and sliced
1 yellow pepper, deseeded
   and sliced
2 garlic cloves, peeled and grated
2cm (¾in) piece of root ginger,
   peeled and grated
1 tbsp curry powder
½ tbsp ground cumin
1 tbsp fish sauce
½ red chilli, deseeded and chopped
4 tbsp peanut butter powder,
   mixed with 2 tbsp of water
juice of 1 lime
250ml vegetable stock
   (1 vegetable stock cube,
   dissolved in 250ml boiling water)
250ml dairy-free coconut milk
   alternative
sea salt and freshly ground
   black pepper

TO ACCOMPANY *(optional)*
50g uncooked basmati rice per
   portion, cooked according to
   packet instructions (+ 173 kcal
   per 125g cooked serving)

This rich and fragrant Thai curry has a subtle kick of warming spices. It isn't as hot as other red curries from the region but it is still packed with peanut butter and coconut flavours. We've swapped the traditionally high-fat ingredients for lower-fat alternatives to save some calories, which means this creamy coconut curry can be enjoyed guilt free!

Weekly Indulgence

Spray a wok or large frying pan with low-calorie cooking spray, place over a medium heat and fry the tofu for 3–5 minutes until golden on all sides. Put to one side.

Spray the wok or frying pan with a little more low-calorie cooking spray and fry the onions and carrots for 5–10 minutes until they soften, then add the peppers, garlic and ginger and fry for a further 3–5 minutes. Add the curry powder, cumin, fish sauce, chilli, peanut butter, lime juice, stock and coconut milk alternative and cook for 10 minutes, stirring occasionally until the sauce has thickened a little. Add the tofu to the sauce and simmer for about 5 minutes until piping hot.

Season and serve. You can also freeze the curry to have another day.

SWAP THIS: Swap the tofu for extra vegetables or Quorn pieces.

TIP: You can get a better texture from your tofu if, before you cut it, you wrap it in kitchen towel and place a heavy pan on top. This will remove all excess liquid, resulting in firmer tofu.

SWEDISH MEATBALLS

🕐 **15 MINS**　　🍲 **25 MINS**　　✕ **SERVES 4**

F

PER SERVING:
365 KCAL / 12G CARBS

500g 5%-fat beef mince
250g 5%-fat pork mince
1 onion, peeled and finely diced
60g wholemeal breadcrumbs
1 tsp ground cumin
½ tsp ground allspice
½ tsp ground nutmeg
3 medium egg yolks
sea salt and freshly ground
　black pepper
low-calorie cooking spray
500ml beef stock (1 beef stock pot
　dissolved in 500ml boiling water)
1 tsp light soy sauce
1 tsp Dijon mustard
40g reduced-fat cream cheese
4g fresh parsley leaves, chopped

TO ACCOMPANY *(optional)*
Cauliflower Cheese and Potato
　Mash, page 211 (+ 248 kcal
　per serving)

Our take on a popular meatball dish uses lower-fat ingredients such as 5%-fat pork and beef mince to keep the calories low. The meatballs are simmered in a creamy Dijon sauce made with reduced-fat cream cheese to create a wonderfully rich flavour.

Special Occasion

Preheat the oven to 220°C (fan 200°C/gas mark 7). Place the minced beef, minced pork and onion in a large bowl and mix well. Add the breadcrumbs, cumin, allspice, nutmeg, egg yolks and mix until combined. Season with salt and pepper. To check the seasoning, fry a small amount of mixture, taste and add more salt and pepper if needed.

Divide the mixture into twenty equal-sized meatballs. Spray a large frying pan with low-calorie cooking spray and place over a medium heat. Fry the meatballs for 4–5 minutes, turning to seal on all sides. Transfer the meatballs to an ovenproof dish and place in the oven for 10 minutes until cooked.

While the meatballs are cooking, add the stock, soy sauce and Dijon mustard to the same frying pan that you cooked the meatballs in. Simmer for 4–5 minutes until it has reduced slightly.

Add the reduced-fat cream cheese and half of the parsley to the frying pan and stir well. Add the meatballs to the sauce and simmer for a further 8–10 minutes. Add a splash of water to thin out the gravy. Season to taste if needed. Sprinkle with the remaining parsley and serve. If you are making the dish for another day, allow to cool first before freezing.

TIP: To boost the Scandinavian feel, add thinly sliced cucumber and a sprinkling of chopped dill fronds, and serve with cranberry sauce.

CHICKEN *and* PINEAPPLE STIR-FRY

🕐 **10 MINS**　🍲 **15 MINS**　✕ **SERVES 4**

Ⓕ ⓖⒻ *use GF soy sauce*

PER SERVING:
211 KCAL / 14G CARBS

low-calorie cooking spray
500g diced chicken breast (skin
   and visible fat removed)
½ red onion, peeled and sliced
½ red pepper, deseeded
   and sliced
½ green pepper, deseeded
   and sliced
1 tbsp soy sauce
1 tbsp rice vinegar
½ tsp garlic granules
1 tsp Sriracha sauce
2 tsp granulated sweetener
320g fresh pineapple, cored,
   skin removed and chopped
4 spring onions, trimmed and sliced
sea salt and freshly ground
   black pepper

TO ACCOMPANY *(optional)*
50g uncooked basmati rice per
   portion, cooked according to
   packet instructions (+ 173 kcal
   per 125g cooked serving)

A vegetable-packed chicken stir-fry with a tropical twist. Our version is a quick and easy fakeaway that's slimming friendly, perfect for a Friday night treat.

Everyday Light ──────────────────

Spray a large frying pan with low-calorie cooking spray and place over a medium heat. Add the diced chicken and fry for 5 minutes until it is browned on all sides. Add the red onion and peppers and fry for a further 5 minutes until softened.

Place the soy sauce, rice vinegar, garlic granules, sriracha and granulated sweetener into a small bowl and mix until combined.

Add the pineapple to the frying pan and pour over the sauce. Stir until the chicken and vegetables are coated in the sauce and cook for 4–5 minutes until the sauce has thickened and become sticky.

Stir the spring onions through, season to taste and serve. You can also freeze the dish once cooled for another day – just remember to defrost thoroughly before reheating.

TIP: You can use tinned pineapple, but this will increase the calories to 218 kcal per portion.

CHICKEN SHASHLIK

🕐 **10 MINS**   🍲 **20 MINS**   ✕ **SERVES 4**

F GF  *use GF soy sauce*

PER SERVING:
239 KCAL / 9.2G CARBS

FOR THE KEBABS
650g skinless chicken breast,
  cut into small chunks
50g fat-free natural or
  Greek yoghurt
1 tbsp soy sauce (dark or light)
2 tsp garlic granules
1 tsp paprika, plus extra to serve
1 tsp ground ginger
1 tsp chilli powder (adjust to taste)
low-calorie cooking spray

FOR THE VEGETABLES
3 peppers, deseeded and sliced
2 onions, peeled and thinly sliced
150ml water
2 tsp garlic granules
2 tsp ground coriander
1 tsp paprika, plus extra to serve
sea salt and freshly ground
  black pepper

TO ACCOMPANY *(optional)*
50g fat-free Greek yoghurt
  (+ 29 kcal per serving) and
  50g uncooked basmati rice
  per portion, cooked according
  to packet instructions
  (+ 173 kcal per 125g cooked
  serving) or a low-calorie tortilla
  wrap (+ 104 kcal per serving)

SWAP THIS: Use pork
instead of chicken, or swap
chicken breast for skinless
boneless chicken thighs.

Tasty skewers of marinated chicken with colourful vegetables are a true takeaway classic. In our version of this versatile dish, we cook the veggies and meat separately so both will be perfectly tender and delicious!

Weekly Indulgence

Preheat the oven to 240°C (fan 220°C/gas mark 9).

Put the chicken pieces in a bowl, add the remaining kebab ingredients and mix well so that the chicken is coated in the yoghurt and spices. You can cover and marinate the mix for a few hours or overnight in the fridge, but it's okay to cook straight away too!

Assemble the kebabs by threading the meat onto the skewers so that you have eight evenly sized kebabs. Line a baking tray with foil and spray well with low-calorie cooking spray. Lay the kebabs onto the foil and place into the hot oven for 20 minutes. When cooked the chicken will be white throughout.

While the kebabs are in the oven, add the peppers, onions, water, garlic, coriander and paprika to a medium frying pan. Place over a high heat and cook for about 15 minutes until the vegetables are softened and glossy and there is no liquid left in the pan. Lower the heat to medium and cook the vegetables for another 5 minutes until the onions have browned a little. The onions should be soft and smell sweet and caramelized when they are ready. Set aside while you take the kebabs out of the oven.

Serve the kebabs with the vegetables and a side of your choice. You can also cool and freeze the chicken shashlik for another day, remembering to defrost thoroughly before reheating.

TIP: If you use wooden skewers, make sure you soak them in water for 20 minutes before you assemble the kebabs to prevent them burning in the oven.

HONEY CHILLI PORK

🕐 **10 MINS**　　🍲 **2½–3 HOURS**　　✕ **SERVES 4**

use GF stock cubes and GF soy sauce ↗

PER SERVING:
282 KCAL / 13G CARBS

2 tbsp clear honey

¼ tsp dried chilli flakes

1 chicken stock cube, crumbled

3 tbsp reduced-salt dark
   soy sauce

1½ tsp garlic granules

½ tsp ground ginger

juice of 1 lime

low-calorie cooking spray

550g pork tenderloin fillet

4 spring onions, trimmed
   and sliced, plus extra to serve
   (optional)

¼ red chilli, thinly sliced, to serve

TO ACCOMPANY *(optional)*

50g uncooked basmati rice per
   portion, cooked according to
   packet instructions (+ 173 kcal
   per 125g cooked serving)

> **TIP:** This dish can also be cooked in the oven. Spray an ovenproof dish with low-calorie cooking spray, add the pork and the sauce and cover tightly with foil. Bake in a preheated oven at 220°C (fan 200°C/gas mark 7) for 45 minutes, turning the pork over once and basting occasionally. Remove and set the pork aside. Pour the liquid from the dish into a saucepan, add the spring onions and simmer for 10 minutes, until thickened. Cut the pork into eight slices and serve, topped with the sauce.

This dish is inspired by Oriental flavours and combines tender, slow-cooked pork with a delicious, sticky sauce. Great for a fakeaway Saturday night in, as you can leave it cooking for a few hours in the slow cooker while you go out, then enjoy a really tasty meal in the evening with no fuss!

Weekly Indulgence

In a small bowl, mix together the honey, chilli flakes, stock cubes, soy sauce, garlic granules, ginger, lime juice and 2 tbsp of water.

Spray the pot of a slow cooker with low-calorie cooking spray. Place the pork in the bottom of the slow cooker and pour over the sauce mixture. Cover with the lid and turn the slow cooker onto the low setting. Cook for 2½–3 hours.

Turn the pork over once halfway through cooking and replace the lid. Don't lift the lid any more than this, as every time you do, it will lengthen the cooking time by 30 minutes! Remove the pork and wrap it in foil to keep warm.

Pour the sauce from the slow cooker into a small saucepan and add the spring onions. Place the saucepan over a medium heat and simmer, uncovered, for around 10 minutes until the sauce has reduced slightly.

Slice the pork into eight slices and place on a serving dish. Pour the sauce over the sliced pork and serve. Garnish with extra sliced spring onions if you wish, and sliced chilli on the side.

If you are making the dish to freeze for another day, allow to cool first and remember to defrost thoroughly before reheating.

CRISPY CHILLI BEEF

⏱ **10 MINS**   🍲 **25 MINS**   ✕ **SERVES 4**

PER SERVING:
349 KCAL /20G CARBS

1½ tbsp self-raising flour
sea salt and freshly ground
  black pepper
500g rump steak, cut into
  thin strips
1 egg, beaten
low-calorie cooking spray
1 red pepper, deseeded and sliced
1 carrot, peeled and cut into
  thin strips
½ onion, peeled and sliced
5 spring onions, trimmed
  and chopped
2 good pinches of dried chilli
  flakes, or ½ chopped red chilli,
  deseeded
2 garlic cloves, peeled and
  finely chopped
1.5cm (just over ½in) piece of root
  ginger, peeled and finely chopped
juice of 1 lime
2 tsp granulated sweetener
6 tbsp soy sauce (dark soy sauce
  works well, but light is fine too)
3 tbsp rice vinegar
1 tsp honey
2 drops Frank's RedHot Buffalo
  Wings, or another hot/chilli sauce
100ml beef stock
  (½ beef stock cube dissolved in
  100ml boiling water)

TO ACCOMPANY *(optional)*
80g steamed vegetables
  (+ 38 kcal) or 50g uncooked
  basmati rice per portion, cooked
  according to packet instructions
  (+ 173 kcal per 125g cooked serving)

Don't be put off by the ingredients in this one – it's well worth it and tastes as good as it looks! Mouth-watering tender strips of beef in a crispy coating tossed in a rich sauce, full of Asian flavours. Traditionally, this dish is fried in a wok with lots of oil to crisp up the beef strips, so we've baked them instead for a lower-fat twist with all of the flavour.

Special Occasion ─────────────

Preheat the oven to 220°C (fan 200°C/gas mark 7).

Place the flour in a shallow bowl. Season the strips of beef with salt and pepper, dip each one into the beaten egg, then quickly drag it through the flour to give a light coating. Place each piece of coated beef on a baking tray sprayed with a fair bit of low-calorie cooking spray, then give the strips a spray too. You could even put them on a piece of baking parchment to ensure they don't stick. Cook for 20–25 minutes, until the beef is crispy. You can turn them over towards the end if needed.

While the beef is cooking, spray a wok or large frying pan with some low-calorie cooking spray. Over a medium-hot heat, fry the pepper, carrot, onion, spring onions, chilli flakes, garlic and ginger. Cook for 5 minutes, then add the lime juice, granulated sweetener, soy sauce, rice vinegar and honey. Stir, then add a couple of drops of Frank's sauce and the 100ml of beef stock.

Allow to cook for a minute then add the cooked beef strips. Stir well and serve with your choice of accompaniment.

TIP: Leave it until the last minute to add the beef strips to the sauce so they will stay crispy for a bit longer.

A CHICKEN'S VINDALOO

🕐 **15 MINS** (PLUS MARINATING TIME)   🍲 **1 HOUR**   ✕ **SERVES 4**

(F) (GF) *use GF stock cubes* ↗

PER SERVING:
335 KCAL / 24G CARBS

500g diced chicken thighs

FOR THE SPICE MIX
1 tbsp mild chilli powder
1 tsp freshly ground black pepper
½ tsp ground coriander
½ tsp ground turmeric
½ tsp ground cinnamon
1 tsp ground cumin
1 tsp sea salt

FOR THE SAUCE
low-calorie cooking spray
4 onions, peeled and finely chopped
4 garlic cloves, peeled and crushed
35g piece of root ginger,
   peeled and finely chopped
75ml cider vinegar
1 x 400g tin chopped tomatoes
400ml chicken stock
   (2 chicken stock pots dissolved in
   400ml boiling water)
1 tbsp brown granulated sweetener
2 tbsp tomato puree
8 cardamom pods

TO ACCOMPANY *(optional)*
Bombay Potatoes, page 202
   (+ 167 kcal per serving)

If you love curry, but you're not a fan of really spicy food, then 'A Chicken's Vindaloo' is the perfect compromise! Our version of the hot and spicy Indian dish has all of the flavours of a classic Vindaloo, but is much milder to suit all tastes. If the spice level isn't quite right for you, then you can easily make this dish hotter by following the instructions in the tip!

Weekly Indulgence ───────────────

In a small bowl, mix together the chilli powder, pepper, coriander, turmeric, cinnamon, cumin and salt.

Place the chicken on a plate and coat with the spice mix on all sides. Cover with cling film and place in the fridge to marinate for 2 hours.

Spray a large, deep frying pan with low-calorie cooking spray and place over a medium heat. Add the onions and fry, stirring regularly, for 10–15 minutes or until softened and golden brown. Add the garlic, ginger and chicken and fry for 5–10 minutes to seal the chicken. Add the vinegar, tomatoes, chicken stock, brown sweetener, tomato puree and cardamom pods and stir well.

Simmer, uncovered, for 35 minutes, until the chicken is cooked and the sauce has reduced and thickened slightly.

Remove the cardamom pods before serving.

▌ **SWAP THIS:** Swap the chicken thighs for chicken breast or Quorn 'chicken' fillets, or use pork instead of chicken.

▌ **TIP:** To make this curry hotter, add 2 finely chopped, medium green chillies and an extra ½ tbsp mild chilli powder to the onions as you're frying them.

ZINGY CHICKEN SALAD

🕐 **10 MINS** 🗑 **40 MINS** ✕ **SERVES 4**

F **GF** *use GF tortilla chips*

PER SERVING:
211 KCAL / 6.9G CARBS

low-calorie cooking spray
30g chilli Doritos
1 tsp chilli powder
1 tsp garlic granules
1 tsp paprika
1 tsp onion granules
4 chicken breasts (skin and
   visible fat removed)
1 tsp cornflour
1 egg

TO ACCOMPANY *(optional)*
75g mixed salad (+ 15 kcal per
   serving) or Coleslaw, page 220
   (+ 80 kcal per serving)

One of our favourite fast-food choices used to be the crispy-coated spicy chicken burger. Our version has it all, and you will love how we get the crunchy coating! Irresistible and lower in calories, this burger is just like the real thing and so simple to make. You can also change the spice mix to suit your taste, so if you prefer some extra 'zing' then add a little more chilli powder.

Everyday Light ────────────────

Preheat the oven to 180°C (fan 160°C/gas mark 4) and spray a baking tray with low-calorie cooking spray. Place the Doritos and spices into a food bag and smash until they are nearly all in a fine crumb, but some larger pieces remain.

Ensure the chicken breasts are dry. Dust lightly with the cornflour. Break the egg into a dish and dip each chicken breast into it. Put the chicken breasts onto the baking tray and sprinkle over the spice and Dorito mix, ensuring both sides of the chicken are coated thoroughly. Spray liberally with low-calorie cooking spray and bake in the oven for 25 minutes.

After 25 minutes, turn the chicken and spray with low-calorie cooking spray again. Bake for a further 15 minutes until the chicken is completely cooked through and golden.

Serve with your choice of garnish. (You can also make your zingy burgers in advance and pop them in the freezer once they have cooled to have later. Remember to defrost thoroughly before reheating.)

TIP: We like to serve this with our Quick Ketchup (page 39) on the side.

STIR-FRIED BEEF *with* GINGER *and* SPRING ONION

🕐 **15 MINS** 🍲 **15 MINS** ✕ **SERVES 4**

use GF soy and oyster sauce ↗

F **GF**

PER SERVING:
309 KCAL /15G CARBS

low-calorie cooking spray
500g rump/sirloin/fillet/topside beef, thinly sliced
2 tbsp rice vinegar
1 onion, peeled and sliced
2 garlic cloves, finely chopped
2cm (¾in) piece of root ginger, peeled and finely chopped
5 large mushrooms, sliced
80ml oyster sauce
3 tbsp soy sauce (dark soy sauce works well, but light is fine too)
1 tsp granulated sweetener (optional)
4 spring onions, trimmed and sliced
1 red pepper, deseeded and sliced
1 yellow pepper, deseeded and sliced
1 green pepper, deseeded and sliced
5 baby corn

TO ACCOMPANY *(optional)*
50g uncooked basmati rice per portion, cooked according to packet instructions (+ 173 kcal per 125g cooked serving)

This dish is the perfect Chinese fakeaway as it's much lower on calories and fat, but packed full of flavour. If you prefer, you could swap the beef for pretty much any meat, including pork, or even prawns instead. The ginger flavour is quite mellow in this dish, so if you're a big fan of ginger, then feel free to add a bit more in order to give it a bigger kick!

Weekly Indulgence

Spray a large frying pan or wok with some low-calorie cooking spray and gently heat. Brown the beef on both sides in small batches. You just want to colour the beef – DO NOT let it cook through! Set aside once done.

Deglaze the pan with 1 tbsp of rice vinegar and a bit of water. Make sure you get all the beef that is stuck to the bottom as this will give your dish real depth of flavour. Spray the pan with some more low-calorie cooking spray and fry the onion, garlic, ginger and mushrooms until the onion is soft.

Add the oyster sauce, soy sauce and the remaining rice vinegar and cook until it thickens. If you want, you can also add 1 tsp of granulated sweetener at this point, but this is optional.

Return the beef to the pan along with the chopped spring onions, and cook for a further 5 minutes, stirring often.

Add the peppers and baby corn, and cook for a further 2–3 minutes. Serve and enjoy! (Or you can freeze the dish once cooled to have another day.)

CHINESE CHICKEN
and BROCCOLI

🕐 **10 MINS**   🍲 **20 MINS**   ✕ **SERVES 4**

F GF   *use GF soy sauce, oyster sauce and stock* ↗

PER SERVING:
184 KCAL / 16G CARBS

low-calorie cooking spray
2 chicken breasts (skin and visible
   fat removed), diced
sea salt and ¼ tsp freshly ground
   black pepper
1 white onion, peeled and sliced
1 garlic clove, crushed
½ tsp minced root ginger
200g button mushrooms, quartered
2 carrots, peeled and cut into strips
6 spring onions, trimmed and sliced
1 head of broccoli (cut into small
   florets and slice the stems) or
   1 pack of Tenderstem broccoli
2 tbsp dark soy sauce
2 tbsp oyster sauce
2 tbsp rice vinegar or white
   wine vinegar, with a little
   sweetener added
200ml chicken stock (1 stock cube
   and 1 stock pot dissolved in
   200ml boiling water)

TO ACCOMPANY *(optional)*
50g uncooked basmati rice per
   portion, cooked according to
   packet instructions (+ 173 kcal
   per 125g cooked serving), or 80g
   steamed vegetables (+ 38 kcal)

If you're a fan of Chinese dishes, you'll love this dish. In fact, it's pretty close to how Chinese takeaways taste – only minus the sesame oil and sugar. Colourful vegetables add crunch and together with a deep savoury sauce make this an ideal family fakeaway!

Everyday Light ────────────────

Heat up a wok or decent-sized frying pan and spray with low-calorie cooking spray. Add the diced chicken, season with salt and pepper, and cook for 3–5 minutes until browned. Remove the chicken from the pan and set aside.

Spray your pan with a bit more low-calorie cooking spray, then add the onion, garlic, ginger and mushrooms. Stir and cook until they are browned and starting to soften. Add the carrots, spring onions and broccoli florets.

Return the chicken to the pan. Stir in the dark soy sauce, oyster sauce and rice vinegar. Pour in the stock, stir well and allow to simmer for 8–10 minutes, stirring occasionally, until the sauce reduces and thickens slightly.

Check the chicken is cooked, then serve with an accompaniment of your choice (or you can let it cool and freeze it for another day).

> **TIP:** Don't throw the broccoli stems away! When chopped and added to this dish they give it extra crunch and texture. Be sure to add them to the pan a little earlier than you would the florets as they take a bit longer to cook.

SPICY RICE

🕐 **5 MINS**   🍲 **25 MINS**   ✕ **SERVES 4**

use GF stock

PER SERVING:
397 KCAL / 82G CARBS

low-calorie cooking spray
½ red onion, peeled and finely
  chopped
½ red pepper, deseeded and
  finely chopped
½ green pepper, deseeded
  and finely chopped
½ tsp ground cumin
¼ tsp chilli powder
1 tsp ground turmeric
1 tsp paprika
400g uncooked long-grain rice
1 litre hot chicken (or vegetable)
  stock (1 cube dissolved in 1 litre
  boiling water)
1 chicken (or vegetable) stock pot
70g frozen peas

TO ACCOMPANY *(optional)*
Tex-Mex Meatballs, page 50
  (+383 kcal per serving) or
  Baked Chimichanga, page 57
  (+405 kcal per serving), and
  some lemon wedges

This brightly coloured rice dish is packed full of crunchy vegetables and tastes just like a popular restaurant favourite! This works wonderfully as a side dish to so many meals, including many of our Mexican mains. If you're feeling brave, you can easily add a little more chilli powder for a bigger kick!

Special Occasion ——————————————

Spray a large frying pan with low-calorie cooking spray. Add the chopped onion, peppers, cumin, chilli powder, turmeric and paprika. Cook until the onions start to brown slightly.

Add the rice to the onions and peppers and stir to mix well. Pour in the hot stock, then add the chicken (or veg) stock pot and stir. Bring to the boil then cover with a lid and cook according to the time specified on your rice packet. Stir during cooking to prevent the rice sticking to the pan.

Around 4 or 5 minutes before the end of cooking, stir in the peas and replace the lid. When all the water has been absorbed and the rice is cooked, stir and serve with an accompaniment of your choice. (You can also put it in the freezer to have another day.)

TIP: Whatever you serve this rice with, even if you eat it as is, a little peri-peri hot sauce works a treat.

CHICKEN CHOW MEIN

🕐 **15 MINS**　　🍲 **20 MINS**　　✕ **SERVES 4**

PER SERVING:
359 KCAL / 45G CARBS

low-calorie cooking spray
1 large onion, sliced
1 tsp minced root ginger
1 tsp garlic, peeled and minced
1 large carrot, peeled and cut into
　slim batons
3 chicken breasts (skin and visible
　fat removed), cut into chunks
3 tbsp dark soy sauce
2 tbsp oyster sauce
2 tbsp rice vinegar or the juice
　of 1 lime
1 tsp granulated sweetener
½ tsp freshly ground black pepper
½ tsp Chinese 5-spice
4 nests of egg noodles (about
　150g in total – 38g per nest)
1 red pepper, deseeded and cut
　into slices
1 green pepper, deseeded and
　cut into slices
150g mangetout, chopped in half
6 spring onions, trimmed and
　finely chopped
1 x 200g tin water chestnuts
1 x 200g tin beansprouts

Chow Mein means 'stir noodle', or 'stir-fried noodle'. Our recipe uses egg noodles, tender chicken and veggies and is perfect after a busy day or just when you don't fancy making anything too complicated. Dark soy sauce, rice vinegar, oyster sauce and Chinese 5-spice all combine in this dish for that beautifully familiar Asian flavour.

Everyday Light ─────────────────

Spray a wok with low-calorie cooking spray and fry the onion, ginger, garlic and carrot until they start to become aromatic. Add the chicken breast and cook over a high heat for about 5 minutes until the chicken begins to brown. Add the soy sauce, oyster sauce, rice vinegar, sweetener, black pepper and Chinese 5-spice and stir well. Continue to cook the chicken over a high heat for a further 8–10 minutes. Meanwhile, cook the noodles according to the packet instructions. Drain and set aside.

Add the peppers, mangetout, spring onions and water chestnuts to the chicken and turn down to a simmer. Cook for another 3–5 minutes depending on how crunchy you like the veg. Stir through the noodles and beansprouts and serve.

SWAP THIS: Swap the chicken for another meat, or for any veg you like.

BATCH COOK

CHAPTER 3

CREAMY BOLOGNESE

⏱ **20 MINS** 🍲 **1 HOUR 35 MINS** ✕ **SERVES 4**

F GF use GF stock cubes

PER SERVING:
310 KCAL / 20G CARBS

low-calorie cooking spray
500g extra lean minced beef
1 onion, peeled and diced
4 garlic cloves, peeled and crushed
2 carrots, peeled and cut into
   small dice
1 courgette, cut into small dice
2 peppers, deseeded and cut into
   small dice
1 x 400g tin chopped tomatoes
175ml skimmed milk
1 beef stock cube dissolved in
   250ml boiling water
1 white wine stock pot
a good handful of fresh
   basil, chopped
90g reduced-fat spreadable cheese
sea salt and freshly ground
   black pepper

TO ACCOMPANY *(optional)*
50g uncooked pasta per portion,
   cooked according to packet
   instructions (+ 174 kcal per
   100g cooked serving), and
   15g finely grated Parmesan
   (+ 62 kcal per serving)

Everyone has their own favourite Bolognese recipe, but these seldom resemble the traditional Italian sauce. We were somewhat surprised to discover many traditional recipes called for milk! We experimented and came up with this luscious, creamy dish that's packed with (non-traditional!) veggies in a delicate sauce – Bolognese, but not as you know it! This is great stirred through pasta, but also served on a jacket potato or with some chunky wedges and salad.

Special Occasion

Spray a large non-stick pan with low-calorie cooking spray and place over a medium heat. Add the mince and brown for 5–6 minutes. Add the onion and garlic and continue to cook for another 3–4 minutes. Add the carrots, courgette and peppers, then stir in the tinned tomatoes. Stir in the milk, beef stock and the white wine stock pot (no need to dissolve this in water first, it will dissolve in the pan). Bring to the boil, then reduce the heat to a gentle simmer. Cover and cook for 40 minutes, stirring occasionally.

After 40 minutes, remove the lid and stir in the basil. Continue cooking, uncovered, for another 35–40 minutes. During this time the sauce should reduce. Keep an eye on it and don't let it dry out. Add a little more water if it does.

When cooked, stir in the spreadable cheese and taste. Season with salt and pepper if needed, then serve with pasta or your choice of accompaniment.

SWAP THIS: Try pork or turkey mince instead of mince beef. Leave out the mince and stir in 2 tins of drained lentils at the end.

HOW TO BATCH: Cool the sauce within 2 hours of cooking, then divide it into individual servings and freeze immediately. Find detailed guidelines on reheating on page 13.

CREAMY CHICKEN *and* TARRAGON HOTPOT

🕐 **20 MINS**   🍲 **1 HOUR 25 MINS**   ✕ **SERVES 4**

Tarragon, a versatile herb with a light aniseed and vanilla flavour, works brilliantly in this chicken hotpot! Using light spreadable cheese in the sauce instead of cream means the calories are reduced, too.

PER SERVING:
371 KCAL / 42G CARBS

low-calorie cooking spray
4 chicken breasts, approximately 140g each, cut into 4cm (just over 1½in) pieces
2 onions, peeled and chopped
1 garlic clove, crushed
2 medium celery sticks, trimmed and cut into 2cm (¾in) pieces
2 medium carrots, peeled and cut into 2cm (¾in) pieces
115g swede, peeled and cut into 2cm (¾in) pieces
2 medium potatoes, washed but unpeeled
½ tsp salt
500ml chicken stock (2 chicken stock cubes dissolved in 500ml boiling water)
50g pearl barley, rinsed
5g fresh thyme, finely chopped
10g fresh tarragon, finely chopped
¼ tsp mustard powder
¼ tsp ground nutmeg
30g light spreadable cheese

TO ACCOMPANY *(optional)*
80g steamed vegetables
(+ 38 kcal per serving)

Weekly Indulgence

Spray a large ovenproof pan (with a lid) with low-calorie cooking spray, place over a medium heat, add the chicken and fry for 5 minutes until evenly browned. Remove from the pan and set aside. Add the onions, garlic, celery, carrots and swede to the pan and fry for 10–15 minutes until softened.

While the pan mix is cooking, put the potatoes in a saucepan with enough water to cover. Add ½ tsp salt and par-cook over a medium heat for 10–15 minutes. Remove from the heat, drain, and put the potatoes into cold water to stop them cooking further.

Return the chicken to the ovenproof pan and add the chicken stock, pearl barley, thyme and half the tarragon. Cover and cook for 30 minutes, stirring occasionally.

After 30 minutes, preheat the oven to 210°C (fan 190°C/gas mark 6). Remove the lid from the pan and cook for a further 10 minutes to reduce the liquid by half. Stir in the mustard, nutmeg and spreadable cheese. Remove the pan from the heat and slice the cooked potatoes into rounds. Arrange the sliced potatoes on top of the pan, spray with low-calorie cooking spray, then place in the oven for 20–25 minutes until golden brown.

Sprinkle with the remaining chopped tarragon and serve.

SWAP THIS: Use chicken thighs or Quorn alternative instead of chicken breast, or for a totally vegetable filling, bulk it out with extra veg (e.g. butternut squash) instead of using chicken.

HOW TO BATCH: Cool within 2 hours of cooking (minus the tarragon garnish), then divide the cooked recipe into individual servings and freeze immediately. Find detailed guidelines on reheating on page 13.

CHICKEN MARSALA

🕐 **10 MINS**   🍲 **25 MINS**   ✗ **SERVES 4**

F

PER SERVING:
198 KCAL / 7.3G CARBS

4 small chicken breasts (skin and
   visible fat removed)
1 tbsp plain flour
sea salt and freshly ground
   black pepper
2 tbsp reduced-fat butter
350ml chicken stock (1 chicken
   stock cube dissolved in 350ml
   boiling water)
2 shallots, peeled and finely
   chopped
200g mushrooms, cut into
   chunky slices
2 garlic cloves, peeled and crushed
50ml Marsala wine
small handful of flat-leaf
   parsley, chopped

TO ACCOMPANY *(optional)*
baked potato, 225g uncooked
   (+ 165 kcal per serving)

Loaded with wine and butter, Chicken Marsala isn't something you would typically think of when looking for a calorie-friendly dinner. We've taken this Italian-American favourite and lightened it up while still keeping the essential flavours of butter and wine. You won't be able to tell the difference!

Everyday Light ─────────────────────

Butterfly the chicken breasts. To do this, slice horizontally from the thicker outer edge of the chicken breast, stopping about 1cm (½in) from the other edge of the breast, and fold open like a book. Season the flour with a little salt and pepper and dust each butterflied breast so they have a light coating.

Melt half of the butter in a frying pan over a medium heat and then add the chicken. Cook for 2 minutes each side until golden brown. You may need to do this in two batches, depending on the size of the chicken breasts. When browned, remove the chicken and place to one side.

Deglaze the pan with a little stock, scraping up any crispy brown bits on the bottom. Add the remaining butter and sauté the shallots for a couple of minutes until golden, then add the mushrooms and garlic and continue cooking for another minute. Pour in the Marsala wine and scrape up any more crispy golden bits from the bottom of the pan. Stir in the rest of the chicken stock and bring to a simmer.

Return the chicken to the pan, and cook for 15 minutes, turning it over halfway through. Check your chicken is cooked. There should be no pink in the middle. The sauce should have reduced during the cooking time, but if you find it a little thin, remove the chicken and turn up the heat for a couple of minutes until it has thickened. Return the chicken to the pan, stir in the parsley and serve.

TIP: You can use any mushrooms for this recipe, but we love to use wild mushrooms.

HOW TO BATCH: Cool within 2 hours of cooking, then divide the cooked recipe into individual servings and freeze immediately. Find detailed guidelines on reheating on page 13.

CHICKEN CHASSEUR

🕐 **15 MINS**　　🍲 **1 HOUR 25 MINS**　　✕ **SERVES 4**

F **GF** *use GF stock cube* ↗

PER SERVING:
330 KCAL / 16G CARBS

low-calorie cooking spray
4 medium chicken breasts
    (skin and visible fat removed),
    about 140g each
180g shallots, peeled and chopped
2 garlic cloves, peeled and
    finely chopped
200g button mushrooms, halved
6 smoked bacon medallions,
    cut into strips
2 medium carrots, peeled
    and chopped
100g celery, trimmed and chopped
2 tbsp white wine vinegar
2 tbsp tomato puree
1 x 400g tin chopped tomatoes
2 bay leaves
1 tsp dried parsley
1 tsp dried thyme
10g fresh tarragon, chopped
200ml vegetable stock
    (1 vegetable stock cube
    dissolved in 200ml boiling water)
sea salt and freshly ground
    black pepper

TO ACCOMPANY *(optional)*
baked potato, 225g uncooked
    (+ 165 kcal per serving)

This recipe is based on a French bistro classic. Tender pieces of chicken lovingly simmered with mushrooms, tomatoes and tarragon until the flavours fuse. We have kept the calories low by skipping the red wine you'd traditionally find in this dish, but it's so flavourful you won't even miss it!

Weekly Indulgence

Preheat the oven to 200°C (fan 180°C/gas mark 6).

Spray a large frying pan with low-calorie cooking spray and place on a medium to high heat. When hot, fry the chicken breasts for 2–3 minutes on each side until golden, then place the chicken in an ovenproof dish.

Reduce the heat to medium, then add the shallots, garlic, mushrooms and bacon to the frying pan and cook for 5 minutes.

Add the carrots and celery and cook for a further 5 minutes, then add the white wine vinegar, tomato puree and tomatoes. Stir and cook for 2 minutes.

Add the bay leaves, parsley, thyme and half of the tarragon along with the vegetable stock and simmer for 5 minutes.

Pour the vegetables and sauce over the chicken and cover with foil, then transfer to the oven. Cook for 25 minutes, then remove the foil and cook for a further 40 minutes until chicken and vegetables are fully cooked. (At this point you can cool and freeze the chasseur for another day. Defrost thoroughly before reheating.)

Season to taste with salt and pepper. Sprinkle with the remaining tarragon and serve.

SWAP THIS: Swap the chicken breast for chicken thighs.

HOW TO BATCH: Cool within 2 hours of cooking, then divide the cooked recipe into individual servings and freeze immediately. Find detailed guidelines on reheating on page 13.

PULLED CHICKEN BAKED SLIDERS

🕐 **15 MINS**   🍲 **1 HOUR 30 MINS**   ✕ **SERVES 9**

PER SERVING:
296 KCAL / 34G CARBS

3 skinless chicken breasts,
about 140g each
30g BBQ seasoning
low-calorie cooking spray
1 onion, peeled and chopped
1 red pepper, deseeded and
chopped
⅓ red chilli, deseeded and
finely chopped
3 garlic cloves, peeled and minced
1 tbsp tomato puree
1 x 400g tin chopped tomatoes
2 tbsp white wine vinegar
1 tbsp paprika
1 tsp ground black pepper
1 tbsp dried thyme
400ml chicken stock (1 chicken
stock cube dissolved in 400ml
boiling water)
sea salt and freshly ground
black pepper
9 x 60g wholemeal bread rolls,
sliced in half
9 reduced-fat processed cheese
slices
20g reduced-fat spread
small sprig of parsley, chopped

TO ACCOMPANY (optional)
75g mixed salad (+ 15 kcal
per serving)

> **HOW TO BATCH:** The pulled
> chicken mixture can be frozen.
> Cool within 2 hours of cooking,
> then freeze immediately. Allow
> to defrost thoroughly and reheat
> in the oven or microwave before
> assembling the sliders as above.

Cheesy pulled chicken in a lightly spiced sauce, stuffed into a garlic wholemeal roll and baked in the oven – sounds like our idea of heaven! This dish is the perfect crowd pleaser for any barbecue, party or sporting event, and is guaranteed to put a smile on everyone's face. Serve with a fresh side salad for a super indulgent meal that's low on calories!

Everyday Light

Coat the chicken with the BBQ seasoning in a bowl.

Spray a large frying pan with low-calorie cooking spray, place over a medium heat, add the chicken and cook for 5 minutes on both sides until golden brown. Put the chicken to one side.

If needed, spray the pan with more low-calorie cooking spray, then fry the onion, pepper, chilli, and two-thirds of the garlic for 10 minutes or until soft. Add the tomato puree, tinned tomatoes and vinegar, and stir. Add the paprika, black pepper, thyme and chicken stock, and cook for a further 5 minutes.

Place the chicken back in the pan and cook uncovered over a medium heat for 40–50 minutes. When the chicken is cooked, remove from the sauce. Preheat the oven to 200°C (fan 180°C/gas mark 6). Leave the sauce on the heat and pull the chicken apart using two forks. Reduce the sauce by half, then remove from the heat and gently mix in the pulled chicken. Season to taste with salt and pepper.

Place the bottom half of the wholemeal rolls on an oven tray and top with the pulled chicken mixture. Add the reduced-fat cheese slices and replace the tops of the rolls.

In a microwaveable bowl, microwave the reduced-fat spread until just melted, then stir in the remaining garlic and parsley. Brush this mixture over the top of the rolls evenly. Place the tray in the oven and cook for 10 minutes, covering with tin foil to stop the rolls colouring too much. Serve.

SALISBURY STEAK

🕐 **15 MINS**   🍲 **45 MINS**   ✕ **SERVES 4**

PER SERVING:
274 KCAL / 16G CARBS

FOR THE SALISBURY STEAK
1 courgette, grated
1 carrot, peeled and grated
500g 5%-fat minced beef
1 small onion, peeled and
   finely chopped
½ tsp dried oregano
2 tsp mustard powder
1 tsp garlic granules
1 egg, lightly beaten
20g panko breadcrumbs
sea salt and freshly ground
   black pepper
low-calorie cooking spray

FOR THE GRAVY
low-calorie cooking spray
½ red onion, peeled and
   thinly sliced
200g mushrooms, sliced
1 tsp tomato puree
2 tsp Henderson's relish or
   Worcestershire sauce
1 tsp balsamic vinegar
400ml beef stock (1 beef stock pot
   dissolved in 400ml boiling water)
1 tbsp cornflour mixed with
   2 tsp cold water

TO ACCOMPANY *(optional)*
steamed mixed vegetables
   (+ 38 kcal per serving)

Salisbury steak is named after nineteenth-century doctor James Salisbury who recommended it as an aid to digestive problems. Minced beef patties served in a rich mushroom and onion gravy, with added hidden veggies for flavour as well as fibre. We can't claim they will cure any ailments, but we can promise a plate of comforting deliciousness!

Everyday Light ────────────────────

Place the grated courgette and carrot in a clean tea towel and squeeze to remove any excess moisture. Place in a large mixing bowl along with the mince, finely chopped onion, oregano, spices, egg and the panko breadcrumbs and mix until well combined. Season the mix with salt and pepper. You can check your seasoning by cooking a small two pence-size piece in your frying pan to taste and adjust the salt and pepper accordingly.

When you are happy with the seasoning, divide the mix into four equal portions and shape into oval-shaped patties, about 2cm (¾in) thick.

Spray a large frying pan (which has a tightly fitting lid) with low-calorie cooking spray and fry the Salisbury steaks over a medium to high heat for 2–3 minutes each side, until sealed and browned. Be careful turning them over, the added vegetables can make them delicate. It may be easier to cook the steaks in two batches.

Set the sealed patties aside on a plate, and give the frying pan a wipe. Spray the pan with low-calorie cooking spray and over a medium to high heat, sauté the sliced onion for 6–7 minutes until browned. Add the sliced mushrooms, increase the heat to high, and cook for a further 3–5 minutes, stirring all the time, until they soften.

Continued...

SALISBURY STEAK ... *Continued*

Stir in the tomato puree, Henderson's relish or Worcestershire sauce, balsamic vinegar, and the stock. Bring to a simmer and then pour in the cornflour and water mix to thicken the gravy.

Return the Salisbury steaks to the pan and cover. Cook for 15 minutes. Stir and carefully turn the steaks halfway through. After 15 minutes, remove the lid and simmer uncovered for another 5 minutes, until the steaks are cooked through and the gravy has a coating consistency.

Serve with your choice of accompaniment. We recommend steamed vegetables.

HOW TO BATCH: Cool the patties and gravy within 2 hours of cooking, then divide the cooked recipe into individual servings and freeze immediately. Find detailed guidelines on reheating on page 13.

MONGOLIAN BEEF

🕐 **10 MINS**   🍲 **3 HOURS**   ✕ **SERVES 2**

F GF *use GF soy sauce*

PER SERVING:
500 KCAL / 23G CARBS

600g beef stir-fry strips
1 tbsp cornflour
15g piece of root ginger, peeled
    and grated
3 garlic cloves, peeled and grated
75ml soy sauce
2 tsp Sriracha sauce
10g sweetener or sugar
1 small bunch of spring onions,
    trimmed and sliced
200ml water
1 medium carrot, peeled
    and grated
10g sesame seeds
¼ red chilli, thinly sliced
pinch of fresh coriander leaves

TO ACCOMPANY *(optional)*
50g uncooked basmati rice per
    portion, cooked according to
    packet instructions (+ 173 kcal
    per 125g cooked serving)

This recipe is our take on the traditional Chinese restaurant dish of tender strips of beef, coated in a sticky, lightly spiced sauce. Perfect for when you want something that feels naughty, but isn't packed full of extra calories, this dish is a great weekend dinner as you can just pop it in the oven and forget about it for a couple of hours!

Special Occasion

Preheat the oven to 160°C (fan 140°C/gas mark 3).

Place the beef strips and cornflour into a bowl and mix well. Add the ginger, garlic, soy sauce, Sriracha sauce, sweetener, spring onions, water and carrot to the beef. Mix well, then transfer to an ovenproof dish, cover with foil and cook in the oven for 2½–3 hours until the meat is tender and the sauce is thick and glossy.

Serve sprinkled with the sesame seeds, sliced red chilli and coriander leaves.

TIP: You can use more or less sweetener if you prefer, or even sugar, honey or agave syrup. if you are unsure, add a bit, taste and add more if required.

HOW TO BATCH: Cool within 2 hours of cooking, without the sesame seeds, then divide the cooked recipe into individual servings and freeze immediately. Find detailed guidelines on reheating on page 13.

DIJON PORK

🕐 **15 MINS**   🍲 **50 MINS**   ✕ **SERVES 4**

use *GF stock cubes*

PER SERVING:
320 KCAL / 10G CARBS

low-calorie cooking spray
1 onion, peeled and sliced
1 garlic clove, peeled and crushed
575g pork tenderloin, cut into
    12 circular slices
200g button mushrooms, sliced
300ml chicken stock (1 chicken
    stock pot dissolved in 300ml
    boiling water)
3 tbsp Dijon mustard
½ tsp mustard powder
2 tbsp reduced-fat cream cheese
sea salt and freshly ground
    black pepper
2 tbsp chopped flat-leaf parsley

TO ACCOMPANY *(optional)*
50g uncooked basmati rice per
    portion, cooked according to
    packet instructions (+ 173 kcal
    per 125g cooked serving)

This delicious, creamy pork dish is so easy to make that it's sure to become a family favourite! Lean, succulent pork tenderloin, pan-fried with button mushrooms and simmered in a creamy, mustard sauce – it doesn't get much better than that! The creamy sauce is made using reduced-fat cream cheese to keep the calories low without compromising on flavour.

Weekly Indulgence ————————————

Spray a large frying pan with low-calorie cooking spray and place over a medium heat. Add the onion and fry for 10–15 minutes, stirring occasionally, until softened and golden. Add the garlic and slices of pork. Seal the pork for 1–2 minutes on each side.

Add the mushrooms, stock, Dijon mustard, and mustard powder. Stir and simmer uncovered over a medium heat for 25–30 minutes, until the pork juices run clear. Turn the pork over halfway through cooking.

Take the frying pan off the heat and stir in the reduced-fat cream cheese until completely blended. Season to taste. Stir in the flat-leaf parsley and serve immediately.

HOW TO BATCH: Cool within 2 hours of cooking, without the parsley garnish, then divide the cooked recipe into individual servings and freeze immediately. Find detailed guidelines on reheating on page 13.

PEPPERCORN CHICKEN

🕐 **5 MINS**   🍲 **25 MINS**   ✕ **SERVES 4**

use GF stock cubes and Henderson's relish or GF Worcestershire sauce ↗

F **GF**

PER SERVING:
193 KCAL / 2.7G CARBS

low-calorie cooking spray
4 chicken breasts (skin and visible
　fat removed), about 150g each
1 small onion, peeled and
　finely diced
½–1 tsp freshly ground black pepper
½ tsp whole black peppercorns
350ml chicken stock (1 chicken
　stock cube dissolved in 350ml
　boiling water)
1 tsp white wine vinegar
1 tsp Henderson's relish or
　Worcestershire sauce
75g reduced-fat cream cheese

TO ACCOMPANY *(optional)*
Lemon and Garlic Asparagus,
　page 200 (+ 40 kcal per serving)

A rich, creamy sauce with a spicy, peppery kick, packed with succulent chicken breast. This dish is usually made with high-calorie double cream, but our slimming-friendly version uses reduced-fat cream cheese, cutting the calories and fat without compromising on taste.

Everyday Light —————————————

Spray a large non-stick frying pan with low-calorie cooking spray and place over a medium-high heat. When the pan is hot, add the chicken breasts and seal for 2 minutes on each side until nicely golden. Remove from the pan and place to one side.

Give the pan another spray of low-calorie cooking spray, add the onion and sauté for 2–3 minutes until it begins to soften, then add the ground pepper and whole peppercorns and cook for 1 minute. Pour in the stock and add the white wine vinegar and Henderson's relish. Bring to the boil, then stir in the cream cheese, until melted and well mixed in.

Return the chicken to the pan and allow to simmer for 15 minutes, turning the chicken occasionally. Check to see if the chicken is cooked. There should be no pink inside and the sauce should be the consistency of single cream. You can adjust the consistency of the sauce by adding a splash of water to thin it down or by turning up the heat and allowing it to bubble away for a little longer. This will reduce the sauce and thicken it.

When the chicken is cooked through and the sauce is the correct consistency, serve with your choice of accompaniments.

HOW TO BATCH: Cool the chicken within 2 hours of cooking, then divide the cooked recipe into individual servings and freeze immediately. Find detailed guidelines on reheating on page 13.

PIZZA PASTA

🕐 **15 MINS**   🍲 **25 MINS**   🍴 **SERVES 6**

PER SERVING:
390 KCAL /48G CARBS

300g dried pasta
low-calorie cooking spray
1 onion, peeled and diced
1 red pepper, deseeded and diced
1 yellow pepper, deseeded and diced
1 green pepper, deseeded and diced
2 garlic cloves, peeled and crushed
1 x 400g tin chopped tomatoes
1 x 500g carton passata
1 tsp dried oregano
2 tsp Worcestershire sauce (or
   Henderson's relish)
60g sliced pepperoni
7g fresh basil, chopped, plus a few
   extra leaves for garnish
sea salt and freshly ground
   black pepper
140g reduced-fat mozzarella
80g reduced-fat Cheddar

If you love pizza and pasta, why choose just one when you can have both? This pizza pasta is super quick and easy to make; the perfect no-fuss meal to feed the whole family. Combining the classic flavours of a pepperoni pizza stirred through pasta and baked in the oven with a golden bubbly cheese top. A great crowd pleaser!

Everyday Light ————————————————

Preheat the oven to 200°C (fan 180°C/gas mark 6).

Cook the pasta according to the packet instructions, drain and leave to one side.

While your pasta is cooking, spray a large frying pan with low-calorie cooking spray and fry the onion over a medium heat for 3–4 minutes until translucent. Add the peppers and garlic and continue to fry until the peppers are soft. Pour in the chopped tomatoes, passata, oregano and Worcestershire sauce and stir until combined.

Dice 30g of the pepperoni and add to the sauce along with the chopped basil. Season the sauce with salt and pepper to taste.

Tip the cooked pasta into an ovenproof dish, pour over the sauce and stir until the pasta is coated. Sprinkle the pasta with the mozzarella and Cheddar and add the remaining sliced pepperoni to the top of the pasta.

Bake in the oven for 12–15 minutes until the cheese is golden and bubbling and the pasta heated through. Once the pasta is cooked, sprinkle with the fresh basil leaves and serve.

TIP: You could stir half of the cheese into the pasta to make a further layer of cheese. Experiment with extra pizza topping flavours by adding extra ingredients like sweetcorn or pineapple. Make this vegetarian by removing the pepperoni and using Henderson's relish.

HOW TO BATCH: Cool within 2 hours of cooking, without the basil garnish, then divide the cooked recipe into individual servings and freeze immediately. Find detailed guidelines on reheating on page 13.

'The recipes are super easy to make, as the instructions are easy to follow. No fancy ingredients that you have to hunt for. Full of family favourites that everyone will eat.'

JULIE

PHILLY CHEESESTEAK MEATLOAF

🕐 **20 MINS**　　🍲 **1 HOUR 20 MINS**　　✕ **SERVES 4**

PER SERVING:
366 KCAL /18G CARBS

100g potato, washed but peel left
　on, finely grated
low-calorie cooking spray
1 onion, peeled and sliced
2 peppers (any colour will do),
　deseeded and sliced
200g button mushrooms, sliced
2 tbsp white wine vinegar
sea salt and freshly ground
　black pepper
500g 5%-fat beef mince
2 garlic cloves, peeled and
　crushed
1 tbsp mixed herbs
½ tsp ground cumin
1 tbsp sriracha sauce
2 tbsp Henderson's relish
1 tbsp wholegrain mustard
1 egg, beaten
150g light spreadable cheese
150g unsmoked bacon medallions

TO ACCOMPANY *(optional)*
75g mixed salad (+ 15 kcal
　per serving)

HOW TO BATCH:
Cool within 2 hours of
cooking, then divide
the cooked recipe into
individual servings and
freeze immediately. Find
detailed guidelines on
reheating on page 13.

Inspired by one of our favourite American sandwiches, this Philly Cheesesteak Meatloaf has all of the flavours of this classic sandwich, but far fewer calories. Packed full of veg, we've used a light spreadable cheese to keep this dish slimming friendly without compromising on that delicious cheesiness! Serve with a mixed salad and some hot sauce for a really satisfying, tasty meal.

Everyday Light ─────────────

Wrap the grated potato in a clean tea towel and squeeze to remove as much moisture as you can.

For the filling, spray a large frying pan with low-calorie cooking spray and place on a medium heat. Sauté the onion, peppers and mushrooms for 25 minutes, until golden brown and softened.

Stir in the white wine vinegar, season to taste with salt and pepper, and set to one side to cool down. Preheat the oven to 200°C (fan 180°C/gas mark 6).

While the pepper mix is cooling, prepare the meatloaf. Place the beef mince, garlic, mixed herbs, cumin, sriracha, Henderson's relish, grated potato, mustard and egg in a bowl, season and mix thoroughly. Check the seasoning by frying a small piece.

Line a large baking tray with cling film and spread out the mince mix, evenly, to cover the base of the tray. Spread the cheese over the mince. Spread the peppers and onion mix evenly over the cheese, leaving a 1cm (½in) gap around the edges. Roll up into a sausage and shape to completely encase the filling.

Spray a baking tray with low-calorie cooking spray, then remove the cling film and place the meatloaf on the greased tray. Arrange the bacon medallions on top. Place in the oven and cook for 30 minutes, then cover with foil and cook for a further 25 minutes, until the meatloaf is firm to the touch and no longer pink inside.

Remove from the oven and allow to rest for 5 minutes before slicing. Serve with your choice of accompaniments.

CREAMY TUSCAN CHICKEN

⏱ **5 MINS**   🍲 **25 MINS**   ✕ **SERVES 4**

F **GF**  *use GF stock cube*

PER SERVING:
264 KCAL / 13G CARBS

low-calorie cooking spray
500g cherry tomatoes, halved
sea salt and freshly ground
   black pepper
2 onions, peeled and thinly sliced
4 garlic cloves, peeled and minced
4 medium skinless chicken breasts,
   about 130g each
600ml chicken stock (1 chicken
   stock cube dissolved in 600ml
   boiling water)
1 tsp dried basil
¼ tsp dried oregano
180g reduced-fat cream cheese
80g fresh spinach, roughly torn

TO ACCOMPANY *(optional)*
80g steamed vegetables
   (+ 38 kcal) or 50g uncooked pasta
   per portion, cooked according to
   packet instructions (+ 174 kcal per
   100g cooked serving)

With only a handful of simple ingredients, this creamy chicken dish is packed full of flavour and colourful veggies. It goes wonderfully with a number of accompaniments and can go from fridge to table within half an hour, so it's perfect for a midweek dinner!

Weekly Indulgence ——————————————

Preheat the oven to 240°C (fan 220°C/ gas mark 9).

Line a large baking tray with foil and spray with low-calorie cooking spray. Place the tomato halves on the baking tray in a single layer, cut side up. Spray with more low-calorie cooking spray and season with salt and pepper. Roast in the oven for 20 minutes until they have wrinkled a little. Remove and set aside.

While the tomatoes are cooking, spray a large frying pan with low-calorie cooking spray and gently fry the onions and garlic over a medium heat for 5 minutes until they have softened a little. Add the chicken breasts, stock, basil and oregano to the pan. Over a medium heat cook the chicken on one side for 10 minutes. Flip the chicken over, loosely place a lid on the pan and cook for another 10 minutes. It will be ready when the chicken is cooked and white throughout, and the stock has reduced down. You can cut the thickest part of the chicken breast on the underside to check.

Remove the pan from the heat and stir in the cream cheese until it has melted in. If the sauce seems too thin, reduce it over the heat for a bit longer; if it seems too thick, mix in a little water.

Stir the spinach into the sauce so that it wilts slightly, then stir in the roasted tomatoes. Season with salt and pepper to taste and serve with an accompaniment of your choice.

SWAP THIS: Use sundried tomatoes (they won't need cooking but will be much higher in calories) instead of fresh tomatoes, or pork steak instead of chicken.

TIP: We recommend a reduced-fat cream cheese rather than a fat-free one here. The result is a little richer and stands up better to reheating if you plan on batch cooking this recipe.

HOW TO BATCH: Cool within 2 hours of cooking, then divide the cooked recipe into individual servings and freeze immediately. Find detailed guidelines on reheating on page 13.

CHEESEBURGER QUICHE

🕐 **15 MINS**   🍲 **45 MINS**   ✕ **SERVES 6**

F **GF** → *use GF soy and Worcestershire sauce*

PER SERVING:
285 KCAL / 9.7G CARBS

500g 5%-fat beef mince
1 tsp paprika
1 tsp freshly ground black pepper
1 tsp ground cumin
1 tbsp soy sauce
½ tsp sea salt
1 tbsp Worcestershire sauce
low-calorie cooking spray
1 onion, peeled and thinly sliced
2 tbsp white wine vinegar
2 garlic cloves, peeled and chopped
2 tsp granulated sweetener
1 tbsp tomato puree
½ x 400g tin chopped tomatoes
4 eggs
200g reduced-fat cream cheese
100ml semi-skimmed milk
60g reduced-fat Cheddar, grated

TO ACCOMPANY *(optional)*
75g mixed salad (+ 15 kcal
   per serving), gherkins, and 2 tbsp
   store-bought ketchup (+8 kcal
   per serving)

HOW TO BATCH:
Cool within 2 hours of cooking, then divide the cooked recipe into individual servings and freeze immediately. Find detailed guidelines on reheating on page 13.

Our Cheeseburger Quiche combines the flavours of a juicy burger with a quiche to create a dish that's the best of both worlds. We've replaced the pastry crust with a meaty base, topped with a quick tomato sauce, caramelized onions and a cheesy, egg mix. Perfect eaten hot or cold, for a quick lunch or even as part of a picnic.

Everyday Light ─────────────────

Preheat the oven to 200°C (fan 180°C/gas mark 6).

In a mixing bowl, add the minced beef, paprika, black pepper, cumin, soy sauce, sea salt and Worcestershire sauce and mix well. To check the seasoning, cook off a little of the mixture in a frying pan and season some more if needed.

Spray an ovenproof frying pan or 30cm (12in) quiche dish with low-calorie cooking spray, then flatten the mince mix evenly in the base to form a flat disc. Bake in the oven for 10–15 minutes until browned. Remove and drain any excess fat from the dish.

While your mince is cooking, spray a frying pan with low-calorie cooking spray and fry the onion for 15 minutes or until it has caramelized.

In a separate pan, add the white wine vinegar, garlic, granulated sweetener, tomato puree and the ½ tin of tomatoes. Cook over a medium heat until the sauce has thickened.

Spread the tomato sauce evenly over the cooked mince and top with the caramelized onion.

In a bowl, mix the eggs, cream cheese, milk and a pinch of salt and pepper. Pour this mixture into the dish on top of the mince and tomato sauce and top with the grated cheese. Cook in the oven for 20–25 minutes until the egg mix is golden brown and set.

Let the quiche rest for 5 minutes, then slice and serve with your choice of accompaniments.

CREAMY CAJUN CHICKEN PASTA

🕐 **15 MINS**   🍲 **20 MINS**   ✕ **SERVES 4**

use GF pasta and stock cube ↗

F **GF**

PER SERVING:
474 KCAL / 60G CARBS

250g fusilli pasta, or whichever pasta shape you prefer

sea salt

low-calorie cooking spray

2 chicken breasts (skin and visible fat removed), diced (about 120g each)

1 onion, peeled and diced

1 tbsp Cajun seasoning

1 tsp paprika

1 tsp Season All seasoning mix

8 button mushrooms, sliced

2½ peppers, red, yellow and green, deseeded and diced

2 carrots, peeled and cut into thin strips

handful of cherry tomatoes, cut in half

250ml chicken stock (1 chicken stock cube dissolved in 250ml boiling water)

4 spring onions, trimmed and chopped

handful of baby corn, sliced

4 tbsp quark

60g reduced-fat spreadable cheese

2 eggs

freshly ground black pepper

10g grated cheese, to serve

We've packed as many vegetables as we can into our version of this popular recipe to help make it super filling. We've chosen a colourful selection including carrots, peppers and baby corn for added bite, but many other veggies, and even chillies, would also work really well in this dish. Feel free to use up any leftovers and get creative!

Weekly Indulgence ─────────────

Cook the pasta in a large pan of salted boiling water, according to the packet instructions.

Spray a large frying pan with low-calorie cooking spray, place over a medium heat, add the chicken and onion and cook for 3–5 minutes until the chicken starts to brown and the onion starts to soften.

Mix the Cajun seasoning, paprika and Season All seasoning mix together, then add half of it to the pan. Stir and cook for a minute or so. Add the mushrooms, peppers and carrots. Cook for another minute. Add the cherry tomatoes and the chicken stock, followed by the remaining seasoning. Stir well. Cook for about 5 minutes, then add the rest of the vegetables. Stir and cook for another 5 minutes.

In a separate, large bowl (a bowl big enough to accommodate the pasta), mix the quark, spreadable cheese and eggs together until they are smooth, then add the chicken and veg mix. Stir well.

Add the cooked pasta, then serve with some freshly ground black pepper and some grated cheese.

HOW TO BATCH: Cool the dish within 2 hours of cooking, then divide the cooked recipe into individual servings and freeze immediately. Find detailed guidelines on reheating on page 13.

SAUSAGE CASSEROLE

🕐 **10 MINS** 🍲 **5–8½ HOURS** 🍴 **SERVES 6**

F **GF** *use GF stock, Worcestershire sauce and sausages*

PER SERVING:
468 KCAL / 60G CARBS

250ml chicken stock (1 very low-sodium chicken stock cube dissolved in 250ml boiling water)

2 onions, peeled and diced

2 peppers of any colour, deseeded and diced

5 medium carrots, peeled and sliced into thick chunks

600g small potatoes, peeled and cut into big chunks

2 x 400g tins chopped tomatoes

1 tbsp Worcestershire sauce

3 tbsp tomato puree

handful of fresh parsley, chopped

2 garlic cloves, crushed

½ tsp dried oregano

1 tsp dried thyme

1 bay leaf

600g chicken sausages

1 x 400g tin butter beans, drained

1 beef stock pot

pinch of fresh herbs, to serve

Just pop all of these ingredients into the slow cooker and go about your day. When you get home, you'll have a hot, hearty bowl of casserole waiting for you! We've packed ours with veggies and protein-rich beans too, so you can be sure this simple sausage stew will fill you up for longer.

Weekly Indulgence

Put all the ingredients except the sausages, butter beans and stock pot into the slow cooker and stir well. Add the sausages and give a quick stir. Cook on High for 5 hours, or on Low to Medium for 6–8 hours.

Check to make sure all the veg is cooked through. Stir in the butter beans and stock pot. Season to taste. Allow to cook for another 20–30 minutes to heat up the butter beans, then serve, topped with a pinch of fresh herbs.

TIP: You can cook this recipe in the oven in a casserole dish with a tight-fitting lid, or in an oven tray with foil tightly wrapped around the top. Cook for 2–3 hours at 170–180°C (fan 150–160°C/ gas mark 3/4), checking every 30 minutes or so.

HOW TO BATCH: Cool the casserole within 2 hours of cooking, then divide the cooked recipe into individual servings and freeze immediately. Find detailed guidelines on reheating on page 13.

MUSHY PEA CURRY

🕐 **10 MINS**　　📦 **30 MINS**　　✕ **SERVES 6**

use GF stock cubes ↗

PER SERVING:
317 KCAL / 34G CARBS

low-calorie cooking spray
1 onion, peeled and diced
1 garlic clove, crushed
6–8 button mushrooms
2 x 300g tins mushy peas
1 x 400g tin chopped tomatoes
1 x 400g tin baked beans
2 tsp curry powder
1 tsp chilli powder
1 tbsp granulated sweetener,
　or 1 tsp honey
2 chicken stock cubes
500g chicken breast (skin and
　visible fat removed), diced
your choice of veg (we used
　cauliflower, broccoli, carrots,
　green beans and some extra
　mushrooms, but you can use
　whatever you like!)
sea salt and freshly ground
　black pepper
small handful of fresh coriander,
　to serve

TO ACCOMPANY *(optional)*
Simple Naan Bread, page 217
　(+278 kcal per serving)

It might sound like an odd combination, but this dish is an amazing, slimming-friendly substitute for a traditional chip shop curry. It tastes so good that you'll never be tempted by the takeaway version ever again! It's also packed full of veggies and uses loads of store cupboard staples so it's super cheap to make as well.

Special Occasion ───────────────

Spray a large saucepan with low-calorie cooking spray and sauté the onion, garlic and mushrooms over a medium heat for 4–5 minutes. Add the tinned ingredients, curry powder, chilli powder and sweetener/honey and crumble in the stock cubes. Bring to the boil then simmer for 20 minutes.

While this is cooking, sauté the diced meat and all the extra veg in a frying pan, using a little more low-calorie cooking spray. After 20 minutes, remove the curry from the heat and blend until smooth in a food processor.

When smooth, add to the pan with the meat and veg and simmer for another 10 minutes.

Season to taste and serve, scattered with fresh coriander, with your choice of accompaniment.

SWAP THIS:
Use diced pork
instead of diced
chicken breast.

HOW TO BATCH: Cool the curry within 2 hours of cooking, then divide the cooked recipe into individual servings and freeze immediately. Find detailed guidelines on reheating on page 13.

BOLOGNESE RISOTTO

🕐 **5 MINS** 🍲 **30 MINS** 🍴 **SERVES 4**

F **GF** *use GF stock cubes*

PER SERVING:
333 KCAL /46G CARBS

low-calorie cooking spray
1 onion, peeled and chopped into
   small dice
1 carrot, peeled and chopped into
   small dice
1 courgette, chopped into
   small dice
3 garlic cloves
250g lean 5%-fat beef mince
150g Arborio risotto rice
1 x 400g carton passata
2 tbsp tomato puree
1 tbsp dried oregano
1 tbsp dried basil
sea salt and freshly ground
   black pepper
pinch of granulated sweetener
   (optional)
1 litre beef stock (2 beef stock
   cubes dissolved in 1 litre boiling
   water)
4 chestnut mushrooms
pinch of grated Parmesan, to
   serve (optional)
a few basil leaves, to serve
   (optional)

We've combined all of the classic flavours of a spaghetti Bolognese with the rich creaminess of a risotto, so if you like the bol, but not the spag, then this dish will be right up your street! You can use whichever veg you like in this recipe, so if you're not keen on something then you can just replace it with whatever you'd prefer – great for using up leftover veg that you might have lying around!

Everyday Light ───────────────────

Spray a large frying pan with low-calorie cooking spray and place over a medium heat. Add the onion, carrot, courgette and garlic and cook for 2 minutes to soften slightly.

Add the minced beef to the frying pan and brown – this will take around 5 minutes. Once the mince has browned, add the Arborio risotto rice. Combine fully with the veg and meat. Add the passata, tomato puree and herbs, and combine fully. Season to taste – you may need a little pinch of sweetener if it tastes particularly sharp!

Gradually add the beef stock to the frying pan – 250ml at a time is usually enough. Stir frequently and continue to add more stock as it reduces in the frying pan, until you have 250ml of stock remaining. This should take about 15 minutes.

When the rice is almost cooked and you have around 250ml of beef stock left, slice the mushrooms and add to the risotto. Stir to make sure they are covered and then add the remaining stock. Cook for a further 5–6 minutes until the rice is cooked but still has a little bite.

Serve immediately with some Parmesan and basil, if you wish.

HOW TO BATCH: Cool the risotto within 1 hour of cooking, then divide into individual portions and freeze immediately. Find detailed guidelines on storing and reheating rice on page 13.

STEWS
&
SOUPS

CHAPTER 4

CHICKEN TORTILLA SOUP

🕐 **15 MINS**　🍲 **25 MINS**　✕ **SERVES 4**

PER SERVING:
370 KCAL / 39G CARBS

2 skinless chicken breasts,
　about 165g each
1 litre chicken stock (2 chicken
　stock cubes, dissolved in 1 litre
　boiling water)
2 tortilla wraps
low-calorie cooking spray
1 tsp smoked paprika
1 onion, peeled and finely diced
1 red or yellow pepper, deseeded
and cut into 5mm (¼in) dice
3 garlic cloves, peeled
　and crushed
1 fresh chilli, deseeded and
　finely chopped
1½ tsp chilli powder, hot or mild
　depending on your taste
½ tsp ground cumin
1 courgette, cut into
　1cm (½in) dice
1 x 400g tin chopped tomatoes
165g sweetcorn, tinned or frozen
1 x 400g tin black beans,
　drained and rinsed
juice of 2 limes
10g fresh coriander, chopped
2 tbsp fat-free Greek yoghurt,
　to serve
2 spring onions, trimmed and
　thinly sliced, to serve

A warming spicy Mexican soup, traditionally topped with fried tortilla pieces and avocado. In our version, we are saving calories by baking the tortillas, so they are still crisp and ready to soak up the delicious flavours of the soup. We have topped the soup with cooling yoghurt to complete the instantly recognizable Mexican taste!

Everyday Light ────────────────────

Preheat the oven to 200°C (fan 180°C/gas mark 6).

Place the chicken breasts and stock in a medium saucepan, bring to the boil, reduce the heat and poach for 15 minutes.

Cut the tortilla wraps into 1cm (½in)-wide strips, spray with low-calorie cooking spray, sprinkle with the paprika and spread evenly over a baking sheet. Bake in the oven for 10–12 minutes until crisp.

While the chicken and wraps are cooking, you can prepare your vegetables. Spray a saucepan with low-calorie cooking spray and sauté the onion and pepper over a medium heat for 5 minutes. Add the garlic, chilli, chilli powder, cumin and courgettes, and stir well. Pour in the tomatoes and drained sweetcorn.

When the chicken is cooked, remove from the pan. Add a little more water to the cooking liquor to make it up to 1 litre. Add the cooking liquor to the pan of vegetables, stir well and bring to a simmer.

Using two forks, shred the cooked chicken and add to the pan, along with the black beans and the lime juice. Allow to simmer for 10 minutes. (At this point you could allow the soup to cool, to freeze it for another day – defrost it and heat it up, making sure the chicken is heated through, then add your toppings.)

Stir in the coriander and serve in warm bowls, topped with a small dollop of fat-free Greek yoghurt, the spring onions and the crispy tortilla pieces.

SWAP THIS: Swap the chicken for another 400g tin of black beans.

TIP: Use more or less chilli powder, according to how spicy you like it.

HERBY CHICKEN STEW
with DUMPLINGS

🕐 **20 MINS**   🍲 **VARIABLE** (SEE BELOW)   ✕ **SERVES 6**

PER SERVING:
378 KCAL / 48G CARBS

low-calorie cooking spray
500g chicken breast (skin and
    visible fat removed), diced
1 onion, peeled and diced
1 small leek, trimmed and sliced
600g potatoes, peeled and cut
    into 2.5cm (1in) cubes
3 medium carrots, peeled and
    thickly sliced
1 tsp dried thyme
3 chicken stock cubes, dissolved
    in 1.2 litres boiling water for
    stove method and 1 litre for slow
    cooker method
150g self-raising flour
¼ tsp baking powder
sea salt and freshly ground
    black pepper
3 egg yolks
5–6 tbsp water
juice of ½ lemon
1 x 400g tin butter beans,
    drained and rinsed
50g fresh spinach
pinch of chopped parsley, to serve

SWAP THIS:
Use diced chicken
thighs instead of
diced chicken breast.

This comforting, hearty hug-in-a-bowl stew combines
the classic flavours of chicken, lemon and thyme
with fluffy dumplings. Creamy butter beans add extra
fibre and using egg yolks instead of suet makes the
dumplings super light.

Everyday Light

HOB METHOD
🍲 **1 HOUR 25 MINS**

Spray a large saucepan or casserole dish with low-calorie
cooking spray and sauté the chicken over a medium-high heat
for 5 minutes, until sealed. Add the onion and leek and cook for
a further 5 minutes until they begin to soften. Add the potatoes,
carrots and thyme and stir well. Pour in the stock. Bring to the
boil then turn down to a simmer, cover and cook for 1 hour.

Meanwhile, make the dumplings. Sift the flour and baking
powder into a bowl. Add a pinch of salt and pepper, then
the egg yolks. Mix with a fork, then use your hands to rub it in
(as you would using fat), until the mix resembles breadcrumbs.
Add the water, a little at a time, mixing until you have a firm dough.
How much water you use will depend on the size of the egg yolks
(if the dough's too wet, this can result in heavy dumplings). Roll into
six equal-sized dumplings and chill until needed.

After 1 hour of cooking, add the lemon juice, butter beans and
spinach. Stir until the spinach has wilted, then place the dumplings
on top. Cover and allow to simmer for another 15–20 minutes until
the dumplings are risen and fluffy.

Serve, scattered with parsley, and enjoy! (You can freeze the stew
for another day. Allow to cool first before popping into the freezer.
After defrosting later, make sure the chicken is thoroughly heated
through before serving.)

SLOW COOKER METHOD
🍲 4–8 HOURS

Spray a large saucepan with low-calorie cooking spray and sauté the chicken for 3–4 minutes, until sealed. Add the onion and leek and cook for a further 5 minutes until they begin to soften. Place in the slow cooker along with the carrots, potatoes, thyme and stock. Cook on Low for 7–8 hours, or on High for 4–5 hours.

Meanwhile, make your dumplings. Sieve the flour and baking powder into a mixing bowl. Add a pinch of salt and pepper, then add the egg yolks. Mix slightly with a fork, and then use your hands to rub it in (as you would using fat), until the mix resembles breadcrumbs. Add the water, a little at a time, mixing carefully until it comes together into a firm dough. The amount of water that you use will depend on the size of the egg yolks (you're aiming for a firm dough that's not too wet, as this can result in heavy dumplings). Roll into six equal-sized dumplings and then chill until needed.

Half an hour before you are ready to serve, add the lemon juice, butter beans and spinach to the stew. Stir until the spinach has wilted, then place the dumplings on top. Allow to slow cook for a further 25–30 minutes until the dumplings are well risen and fluffy.

Serve and enjoy! (You can freeze the stew for another day. Allow to cool first before popping into the freezer. After defrosting later, make sure the chicken is thoroughly heated through before serving.)

TIP: If you cook it in the slow cooker, it will be ready when you get home after a long day.

Super
EASY

MALAYSIAN FISH CURRY

⏱ **10 MINS**   🍲 **50 MINS**   ✗ **SERVES 4**

GF

PER SERVING:
306 KCAL / 27G CARBS

185g jar Laksa curry paste
400ml unsweetened dairy-free
  coconut milk alternative
400g potatoes, peeled and cut
  into 1.5cm (just over ½in) chunks
700g skinless, boneless cod
  fillets, cut into 4cm (just over
  1½in) chunks
100g fine green beans, trimmed
  and left whole
10g fresh coriander, roughly
  chopped, to serve

TO ACCOMPANY (optional)
50g uncooked basmati rice per
  portion, cooked according to
  packet instructions (+ 173 kcal
  per 125g cooked serving)

A quick and easy Asian-inspired fish curry, flavoured with lemongrass, lime, coconut and coriander, with a slight chilli kick. This is a delicious, fragrant dish that is really simple to prepare and makes a great lunch or dinner. Serve with your choice of accompaniment, but we think it's super tasty when served with basmati rice or egg noodles!

Weekly Indulgence

Heat the curry paste in a medium saucepan over a low heat for 1–2 minutes and stir. Add the dairy-free coconut milk alternative and stir. Add the potatoes, bring to the boil, then lower the heat and cover. Simmer for 20–25 minutes until tender.

Add the fish and gently press down to submerge in the sauce. Do not stir it, otherwise the fish will break up. Cover and simmer on a low heat for 10 minutes.

Add the beans on top of the fish, cover and simmer for a further 10 minutes – again, don't stir to avoid breaking up the fish!

Serve in bowls with a sprinkle of chopped coriander.

SWAP THIS: Use any other curry paste, e.g. Thai, instead of the Laksa curry paste, and swap the cod for any other white fish, fresh or frozen (defrost first).

MUSHROOM BOURGUIGNON

🕐 **10 MINS** 🍲 **45 MINS** ✕ **SERVES 2**

use GF stock cube ↘

V **F** **GF**

PER SERVING:
195 KCAL / 28G CARBS

low-calorie cooking spray
250g chestnut mushrooms,
  roughly chopped
250g small button mushrooms
1 onion, peeled and chopped
1 large carrot, peeled and cut
  into 2cm (¾in) slices
1 garlic clove, peeled and crushed
sea salt and freshly ground
  black pepper
2 tbsp tomato puree
1 tbsp red wine vinegar
1 tbsp balsamic vinegar
1 tbsp Henderson's relish
500ml vegetable stock
  (1 vegetable stock cube dissolved
  in 500ml boiling water)
1 tsp dried parsley
2 tsp dried thyme
pinch of fresh thyme leaves,
  to serve

TO ACCOMPANY *(optional)*
Cauliflower Cheese and Potato
  Mash, page 211 (+ 248 kcal per
  serving)

A veggie twist on the classic French stew, packed full of mushrooms and vegetables in a rich tomato and garlic sauce. Proper winter food that's comforting and warming, perfect for chilly nights when you fancy a hearty meal with minimum fuss!

Weekly Indulgence ───────────

Spray a large frying pan with low-calorie cooking spray and place on a medium heat. Fry the mushrooms for 5 minutes until coloured but firm, place to one side.

In the same pan, add a little more low-calorie cooking spray and fry the onion and carrot for 8 minutes until they start to brown. Add the garlic and cook for a further 2 minutes. Season with salt and pepper. Add the tomato puree, red wine vinegar, balsamic vinegar, Henderson's relish and stock and cook for 20 minutes until the liquid has reduced slightly and the vegetables are soft.

Add the mushrooms back to the pan with the parsley and thyme and cook for 10 minutes more. Check the seasoning and serve, scattered with fresh thyme.

SWAP THIS: Henderson's relish is a gluten-free and vegetarian sauce we often use in place of Worcestershire sauce. If you don't have any dietary requirements you could use Worcestershire sauce instead if you prefer.

TIP: Any mushrooms can be used. If using dried mushrooms, subtract the amount of stock for the amount of water used to rehydrate the mushrooms and use the mushroom stock in the recipe.

MEXICAN STREET CORN SOUP

🕐 **10 MINS**   🍲 **25 MINS**   ✕ **SERVES 4**

use veggie feta cheese

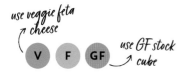

use GF stock cube

PER SERVING:
199 KCAL /28G CARBS

low-calorie cooking spray
1 onion, peeled and diced
1 medium red pepper, deseeded
  and diced
1 green chilli, deseeded and chopped
2 garlic cloves, peeled and crushed
1 medium potato, peeled and diced
1 tsp chilli powder
2 x 200g tins sweetcorn, drained
500ml vegetable stock
  (1 vegetable stock cube dissolved
  in 500ml boiling water)
juice of 1 lime
sea salt and freshly ground
  black pepper
65g reduced-fat feta cheese
10g fresh coriander, chopped,
  to serve

TO ACCOMPANY *(optional)*
4 x 60g wholemeal bread rolls
  (+ 152 kcal per roll)

Inspired by the traditional Mexican street food, *elote*, this Mexican Street Corn Soup has all of the flavours of the grilled corn dish in a creamy and spicy soup. Topped with crumbled reduced-fat feta cheese, this recipe is low on calories but packs a flavour punch!

Everyday Light

Spray a large saucepan with low-calorie cooking spray and place over a medium heat. Fry the onion, red pepper, green chilli and garlic for 5 minutes until soft.

Add the potato, chilli powder, 350g of sweetcorn, stock and lime juice. Bring to the boil and then turn down the heat, cover and simmer for 20 minutes, until the potato is soft.

Add 50g of the reduced-fat feta, then use a stick blender or food processor to blitz the soup until smooth.

Add the remainder of the sweetcorn and season to taste with salt and pepper. Serve with the remaining feta cheese and a sprinkling of coriander on top. (You can cool and freeze the soup for another day, leaving off the garnish till you're ready to defrost and reheat.)

TIP: Loosen the soup with a little water or vegetable stock if you prefer a thinner soup.

'These lovely ladies sat down and said "What do people REALLY want to eat? What do they sacrifice when they are losing weight?" And they came up with healthy versions of all of our favourite things. You can't believe how good they taste until you try them, you'll never eat the fattening versions again.'

~~

MORAG

VEGETARIAN GUMBO

🕐 **15 MINS**   🍲 **55 MINS**   ✕ **SERVES 4**

V F GF *use GF stock cube and soy sauce* ↗

PER SERVING:
144 KCAL /19G CARBS

low-calorie cooking spray

3 medium celery sticks, trimmed
and sliced

1 onion, peeled and cut into chunks

2 garlic cloves, peeled and grated

2 peppers, one green, one red,
deseeded and cut into chunks

200g button mushrooms, left
whole if small, halved if not

2 tsp Cajun seasoning

1 tbsp smoked paprika

½ tsp dried thyme

1 tsp dried chilli flakes

1 tsp dried oregano

2 tbsp tomato puree

1 x 400g tin chopped tomatoes

1 tbsp Henderson's relish

1 tsp soy sauce

1 tsp hot pepper sauce

1 tbsp cider vinegar

2 bay leaves

600ml vegetable stock
(1 vegetable stock cube dissolved
in 600ml boiling water)

170g okra, trimmed and cut into
2cm (¾in) slices

sea salt and freshly ground
black pepper

TO ACCOMPANY *(optional)*

50g uncooked basmati rice per
portion, cooked according to
packet instructions (+ 173 kcal per
125g cooked serving) and 50g
fat-free Greek yoghurt (+ 29 kcal
per serving)

A healthy version of the classic New Orleans dish,
bursting with tender vegetables and thickened
with fresh okra instead of the traditional flour roux.
We've reduced the calories while still retaining all
the delicious spicy flavours of this warming stew.

Everyday Light ────────────────

Spray a large frying pan with low-calorie cooking spray and
place over a medium heat. Add the celery, onion and garlic
and fry for 5 minutes until softened.

Add the peppers and button mushrooms and cook for a further
2 minutes. Add the Cajun seasoning, smoked paprika, thyme,
dried chilli flakes, oregano and tomato puree and cook for
1 minute. Add the chopped tomatoes, Henderson's relish, soy
sauce, hot pepper sauce, cider vinegar, bay leaves and stock
and cook uncovered for 30 minutes.

After 30 minutes, add the okra and cook for a further
10–15 minutes, until the vegetables have softened and the
sauce has thickened.

Season to taste with salt and pepper, remove the bay leaves
and serve with your choice of accompaniments. (Or you can
cool and freeze for another day.)

SWAP THIS: Instead of using okra to help
thicken this stew, add more veg and cook for a
little longer. Use whatever frozen veg you have
(this stew works well with most vegetables).

TIP: For a little
more spice add
an extra ½ tsp
of hot sauce.

LENTIL *and* BACON SOUP

🕐 **15 MINS**   🍲 **30 MINS**   ✕ **SERVES 4**

F **GF**  *use GF stock cubes* ↗

PER SERVING:
237 KCAL / 32G CARBS

low-calorie cooking spray
4 unsmoked bacon medallions,
  cut into 1cm (½in) pieces
1 small onion, peeled and chopped
1 small leek, trimmed and
  thinly sliced
2 medium carrots, peeled and
  finely diced
150g red lentils, rinsed
150g potatoes, peeled and cut
  into 1cm (½in) dice
1 bay leaf
sea salt and freshly ground
  black pepper
1.4 litres ham or chicken stock
  (2 ham or chicken stock cubes
  dissolved in 1.4 litres boiling
  water)
a few sage leaves, finely shredded
  or a pinch of dried sage

TO ACCOMPANY *(optional)*
4 x 60g wholemeal bread rolls
  (+ 152 kcal per roll)

Lentil and bacon is such a classic soup flavour, and for good reason! Lentils are naturally low in fat and high in protein and fibre, while the extra added veg will help to keep you fuller for longer. We've used ham stock cubes in this dish, but if you can't find them, then chicken stock cubes would also work really well.

Everyday Light —————————————

Spray a saucepan with low-calorie cooking spray, place over a medium heat, add the bacon, onion and leek and sauté for 5 minutes until softened. Add the carrots, lentils, potatoes and bay leaf. Season, then stir in the stock. Bring to the boil, then reduce the heat to a simmer. Allow to cook for 20 minutes, then stir in the sage and cook for a further 5 minutes.

Check the seasoning, remove the bay leaf and serve in a warmed bowl. (The soup will freeze well if you want to make it for another day, just allow to cool first).

TIP: This recipe can be cooked in a slow cooker. Once you've stirred in the sage, place all of the ingredients into the slow cooker and turn it on. Cook for 5 hours on High or 7–8 hours on Low. Reduce the amount of stock to 1.2 litres, to account for less evaporation while cooking.

BROCCOLI *and* CHEDDAR SOUP

🕐 **10 MINS** 🍲 **55 MINS** 🍴 **SERVES 6**

  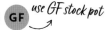 *use GF stock pot* ↗

PER SERVING:
158 KCAL /15G CARBS

low-calorie cooking spray
1 onion, peeled and finely chopped
2 medium leeks, trimmed, washed and sliced
1 garlic clove, peeled and crushed
1 litre vegetable stock (1 vegetable stock pot dissolved in 1 litre boiling water)
300g potatoes, peeled and cut into 2cm (¾in) cubes
pinch of ground nutmeg
sea salt and freshly ground black pepper (a pinch of each)
2 heads of broccoli, cut into florets, about 300g each
120g reduced-fat Cheddar, grated

TO ACCOMPANY *(optional)*
6 x 60g wholemeal bread rolls
   (+152 kcal per roll)

Super comforting and really hearty, this easy Broccoli and Cheddar Soup is so rich and creamy that you'd never believe it's slimming friendly! We've used reduced-fat Cheddar to keep the calories low without compromising on the delicious cheesy flavour. As this soup is also packed full of delicious veg, it'll help to keep you feeling fuller for longer!

Everyday Light

Spray a large saucepan with low-calorie cooking spray and place over a medium heat. Add the onion and fry for 5 minutes while stirring. Add the leeks and garlic and cook for a further 10 minutes, stirring, until softened and golden.

Add the stock, potatoes, nutmeg, salt and pepper. Bring to the boil, lower the heat, cover and simmer for 30 minutes until the potatoes are tender.

Add the broccoli, cover and simmer for 10 minutes or until the broccoli is just tender and still bright green.

Remove the pan from the heat and blend the soup until smooth. Stir in the cheese until melted and season to taste before serving.

TIP: You can also garnish each serving of soup with 5g grated reduced-fat Cheddar for an additional 16 kcal per serving.

CARIBBEAN VEGETABLE STEW

🕐 **20 MINS**   🍲 **30 MINS**   ✕ **SERVES 4**

use GF stock cubes →

VE   F   GF

PER SERVING:
327 KCAL / 55G CARBS

low-calorie cooking spray

1 large onion, peeled and cut
　into large dice

2 peppers, deseeded and cut
　into 2.5cm (1in) pieces

1 chilli, deseeded and
　finely chopped

3 garlic cloves, peeled
　and crushed

½ tsp cayenne pepper

1½ tsp ground allspice

1 x 400g tin chopped tomatoes

400ml dairy-free coconut
　milk alternative

2 vegetable stock cubes

400g sweet potatoes, peeled
　and cut into 2.5cm (1in) chunks

2 medium carrots, peeled and
　cut into 5mm (¼in) slices

2 tsp fresh chopped thyme
　(or use 1 tsp dried thyme)

1 x 400g tin kidney beans,
　drained and rinsed

150g sweetcorn, tinned or frozen

juice of 1 lime

1 spring onion, trimmed and sliced

If you think a hearty stew has to bubble away on the stove for hours and hours before it's ready to eat, think again! Our warming, spicy Caribbean Vegetable Stew takes less than 30 minutes to cook and a bit of chopping is the most difficult part of the entire dish! Not a massive fan of spice? Simply leave the cayenne pepper out if you prefer a milder stew.

Everyday Light ———————————————

Spray a large saucepan with low-calorie cooking spray and place over a medium heat. Add the onion and peppers and sauté for 5 minutes until they begin to soften. Add the chilli, garlic, cayenne pepper and allspice to the pan and stir for 1 minute until fragrant.

Pour in the tomatoes and coconut milk alternative and crumble the stock cubes straight in (you don't have to dissolve them in water first). Stir well and then add the sweet potatoes, carrots and thyme. Bring to the boil, then reduce the heat so that the stew is simmering. Cover and allow to cook for 20 minutes or until the sweet potatoes and carrots are soft.

Stir in the kidney beans and sweetcorn and give them a couple of minutes to heat through. Squeeze in the lime juice, scatter with the spring onion and serve!

TIP: The cayenne pepper gives a spicy kick to this stew. If you don't like too much heat, then just leave it out. This can be cooked in a slow cooker. Just throw all the ingredients except the beans and sweetcorn into the slow cooker and cook on Low for 6–7 hours. Add the beans and sweetcorn half an hour before serving to allow them to heat through.

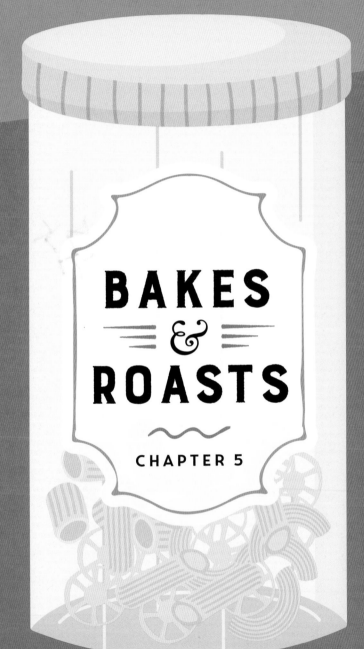

BAKES
&
ROASTS

CHAPTER 5

PORK *and* APPLE TRAYBAKE

🕐 **15 MINS**　🍲 **40 MINS**　✕ **SERVES 4**

PER SERVING:
308 KCAL / 26G CARBS

2 parsnips, peeled and cut into
　large chunks
4 medium carrots, peeled and cut
　into large chunks
1 eating apple
low-calorie cooking spray
2 red onions, peeled and cut into
　thick wedges
4 lean pork steaks or chops,
　trimmed of all visible fat
juice of ½ lemon
½ tsp dried sage
sea salt and freshly ground
　black pepper

TO ACCOMPANY *(optional)*
160g baby potatoes (+ 106 kcal
　per serving)

When Kate was growing up, a regular favourite was baked pork chops, topped with sweet apples, onions and herbs. We've used that as inspiration for this simple traybake, and we've added root vegetables to make this a flavoursome, nutritious family meal.

Weekly Indulgence

Preheat the oven to 200°C (fan 180°C/gas mark 6).

Place the parsnips and carrots in a saucepan, cover with salted water and bring to the boil. Reduce the heat and simmer for 5 minutes, until they are almost cooked, but still firm. Drain well and allow to dry off in a colander while you slice the apple into thick slices.

Spray a large baking sheet with low-calorie cooking spray, and arrange the carrots, parsnips, onions and apple evenly over the tray. Reserve four apple slices. Place the pork chops on the tray, top each with a reserved apple slice, squeeze the lemon juice over the pork and vegetables and sprinkle over the sage. Spray with low-calorie cooking spray and season with a little salt and pepper. Cook in the oven for 30–35 minutes.

Serve with your choice of accompaniment. We love it with baby roast potatoes.

TIP: Don't be tempted to slice the apple in advance, as it will turn brown!

VIKING PORK

🕐 **5 MINS**   🍲 **15 MINS**   ✕ **SERVES 4**

GF *use Henderson's relish* ↗

PER SERVING:
325 KCAL / 3.8G CARBS

low-calorie cooking spray
4 lean pork steaks or chops,
  trimmed of all visible fat
sea salt and freshly ground
  black pepper
1 onion, peeled and finely sliced
160g reduced-fat mature
  Cheddar, grated
1 tbsp Henderson's relish or
  Worcestershire sauce
½ tsp mustard powder
1 egg yolk

TO ACCOMPANY *(optional)*
80g steamed vegetables
  (+ 38 kcal per serving)

Transform a dull pork steak into a delicious dinner with a tangy cheese-and-onion topping. Super quick and easy to make, this country-pub inspired classic will quickly become a family favourite! We're not sure where the Viking name originated, but we think it describes the bold and tangy flavours in this dish, so we kept the name anyway!

Special Occasion ──────────────

Preheat the grill to a high heat.

Spray a baking sheet with low-calorie cooking spray. Season the pork steaks with a little salt and pepper, place on the baking sheet and pop under the grill, turning occasionally until cooked through. This will take around 8 minutes but may take a little more or less depending on the thickness of your pork steaks.

While the pork is cooking, spray a small frying pan with low-calorie cooking spray and place over a medium-high heat. Add the onion and sauté for 5–6 minutes until soft and beginning to brown. When the onion is cooked, place in a mixing bowl with three-quarters of the grated cheese, Henderson's relish, mustard powder and the egg yolk and mix well.

When the pork steaks are cooked, remove from the grill and lower the temperature to medium.

Spread the cheese-and-onion mixture evenly on top of the pork steaks. Sprinkle with the remaining cheese and pop them back under the grill for 5 minutes until the cheese has melted and is golden.

Serve with your choice of accompaniment.

TIP: You could add a pinch of chilli flakes or a dash of hot sauce to the cheese mix if you like things spicy.

HONEY *and* LIME SALMON

🕐 **2 MINS**   🍲 **15 MINS**   ✕ **SERVES 2**

PER SERVING:
283 KCAL / 4.1G CARBS

2 skinless salmon fillets,
  about 120g each
1 lime, or 2 tbsp lime juice
1 tsp soy sauce
1 tsp garlic granules, or 2 garlic
  cloves, peeled and minced
1 tsp honey
freshly ground black pepper

TO ACCOMPANY *(optional)*
80g steamed vegetables
  (+ 38 kcal per serving)

A little sweet and citrusy, this salmon is a quick and easy version of those pre-marinated fish bags you can pick up in the supermarket, perfect for a speedy dinner. You can play around with different seasonings too. How about adding a pinch of chilli powder for a bit of a kick?

Everyday Light ───────────────────────

Preheat the oven to 220°C (fan 200°C/gas mark 7).

Rip off two large pieces of foil, about 30cm (12in) square, big enough for each of the salmon fillets to sit inside. Place a salmon fillet in the middle of a piece of foil. Squeeze over the juice of half a lime (or 1 tbsp), ½ tsp of soy sauce, sprinkle over the garlic granules and drizzle over ½ tsp of honey. You can also season with a little pepper to taste. Scrunch up the foil to seal up the salmon. It will look like a pasty that has been stood up. Repeat with the second salmon fillet.

Place the foil parcels onto a baking tray and into the middle of the hot oven for 15 minutes, until the salmon is cooked and opaque throughout.

Remove from the foil discarding any leftover liquid and serve with an accompaniment of your choice.

SWAP THIS: Swap the salmon for any meaty fish, swap the honey for maple syrup, or swap the lime for lemon.

TIP: You can also leave to cool and use flaked in sandwiches or salads for tasty lunches.

DIRTY MACARONI

🕐 **15 MINS** 🍲 **35 MINS** ✕ **SERVES 6**

PER SERVING:
275 KCAL / 24G CARBS

200g macaroni
low-calorie cooking spray
1 onion, peeled and diced
2 garlic cloves, peeled and chopped
500g 5%-fat pork mince
1 red pepper, deseeded and diced
1 green pepper, deseeded and
  diced
1 tsp dried sage
1 tsp dried oregano
1 tsp dried thyme
1 tbsp Cajun spice mix
1 x 400g tin chopped tomatoes
1 tbsp tomato puree
2 tbsp white wine vinegar
300ml chicken stock (1 chicken
  stock cube dissolved in 300ml
  boiling water)
sea salt and freshly ground
  black pepper
30g wholemeal bread
10g fresh parsley, chopped
40g reduced-fat Cheddar, grated
30g light spreadable cheese

TO ACCOMPANY (optional)
75g mixed salad (+ 15 kcal
  per serving)

Our version of the classic Croatian *Šporki Makaruli* uses lean pork mince and reduced-fat cheeses to keep the calories low. The herbs and Cajun spice give this dish a nice little kick and the crispy, cheesy breadcrumbs take everything to the next level! If you're not a fan of pork, then this recipe would also work really well with lean beef mince instead.

Everyday Light

Preheat the oven to 200°C (fan 180°C/gas mark 6). Place a medium saucepan of boiling water on the hob and cook the macaroni according to the packet instructions. Drain and rinse under cold running water to stop any further cooking. Set aside.

While the pasta is cooking, spray a large frying pan with low-calorie cooking spray, place over a medium heat, add the onion and garlic and fry for 2–3 minutes. Add the pork mince and peppers and fry for a further 5–6 minutes. Add the sage, oregano, thyme and Cajun spice mix and stir. Add the tomatoes, tomato puree, white wine vinegar and chicken stock. Cook for 15 minutes over a medium heat. Season to taste.

Blitz the wholemeal bread using a food processor or mini chopper and place in a mixing bowl. Add the parsley and cheese to the bowl and mix well. Add the spreadable cheese to the pork mixture and mix thoroughly.

Add the cooked macaroni, mix well, then transfer to an ovenproof dish. Top with the breadcrumb-and-cheese mixture and place in the oven for 10 minutes or until the cheese has melted.

Serve. (Or you can cool and freeze to have another day.)

HARISSA *and* HONEY CHICKEN

🕐 **10 MINS**   🍲 **50 MINS**   ✗ **SERVES 4**

PER SERVING:
435 KCAL / 27G CARBS

3 tbsp harissa paste

2 tbsp honey

juice of ½ lemon

1½ tbsp white wine vinegar

8 chicken thighs, boned
  and skinned

2 mixed peppers, deseeded and
  cut into chunks

2 aubergines, cut into chunks

2 red onions, peeled and cut
  into chunks

2 carrots, peeled and cut
  into chunks

2 garlic cloves, peeled
  and crushed

3 sprigs of fresh thyme

½ tsp dried coriander

low-calorie cooking spray

330g fresh cherry tomatoes

sea salt and freshly ground
  black pepper

TO ACCOMPANY *(optional)*
Lime and Coconut Jasmine Rice,
  page 212 (+234 kcal per serving)

Inspired by Middle Eastern and North African flavours, this lightly spiced dish is like summer on a plate! If you've never heard of harissa paste before, then you should be able to find this in a jar with the spices in the supermarket. It can pack a bit of a punch, so if you prefer your food milder, then you may want to reduce the amount of harissa paste that you use!

Special Occasion —————————————————

Preheat the oven to 220°C (fan 200°C/gas mark 7).

In a bowl mix the harissa paste, honey, lemon juice and white wine vinegar. Coat the chicken thighs evenly in the mix. Transfer the chicken to an ovenproof dish and refrigerate for 20 minutes.

In a second ovenproof dish, add the mixed peppers, aubergines, red onions, carrots and garlic.

Add the thyme and coriander to the vegetables and spray with low-calorie cooking spray.

Place both dishes in the oven and bake the chicken and vegetables for 40–45 minutes, remembering to stir the vegetables twice during cooking.

Five minutes before serving, add the cherry tomatoes to the vegetables to warm through. Season the vegetables with salt and pepper to taste.

Place the cooked chicken and all of the juices onto the vegetables and serve. (You can also cool and freeze for another day. Defrost thoroughly before reheating.)

SWAP THIS:
Swap the harissa paste
for a light hot sauce.

'Now I don't have to cook four different meals in the evening as the other half and both of the kids love the Pinch of Nom meals too and will happily eat the same as me.'

KERRY

CHICKEN POT PIE CRUMBLE

🕐 **15 MINS**　　🍲 **1 HOUR 15 MINS**　　✕ **SERVES 4**

PER SERVING:
505 KCAL / 56G CARBS

FOR THE PIE
low-calorie cooking spray
1 onion, peeled and diced
1 celery stick, trimmed
　and diced
1 large carrot, peeled and diced
400g potatoes, peeled and diced
100g frozen peas
1 x 80g tin sweetcorn, drained
700ml chicken stock (1 chicken
　stock cube, dissolved in 700ml
　boiling water)
30g reduced-fat cream cheese
5g fresh parsley, chopped
5g fresh thyme leaves, chopped
400g cooked chicken breast
　(skin and visible fat
　removed), shredded
sea salt and freshly ground
　black pepper

FOR THE CRUMBLE TOPPING
60g oats
35g plain white flour
½ tsp ground black pepper
25g reduced-fat spread
20g reduced-fat Cheddar,
　finely grated

TO ACCOMPANY *(optional)*
80g steamed vegetables
　(+ 38 kcal per serving)

Inspired by a dish we tried on a trip to New York, this creamy chicken and vegetable pie is topped with an oat crumble instead of high-calorie puff pastry. This dish may taste super indulgent, but we've used reduced-fat cheese to keep the calories low without compromising on taste. It's also packed full of veg, so it couldn't be easier to achieve your five a day!

Special Occasion ──────────────────

Spray a large frying pan with low-calorie cooking spray, place over a medium heat and fry the onion, celery and carrot for 10–15 minutes until soft. Add the potatoes, peas, sweetcorn and chicken stock to the frying pan. Cook for a further 15–20 minutes until the potatoes have softened. Add the cream cheese, parsley, thyme and chicken to the pan and mix well. Gently simmer to reduce the sauce by half, around 15 minutes. Meanwhile, preheat the oven to 220°C (fan 200°C/gas mark 7).

Season, then remove from heat and transfer to a medium ovenproof dish.

In a bowl add oats, flour and pepper. Using your fingers, rub in the reduced-fat spread until you have the consistency of breadcrumbs. Add the Cheddar and sprinkle over the chicken mixture.

Place in the oven and cook for 20–25 minutes until the crumble is golden brown.

Serve.

VEGETABLE *and* CHICKPEA ROAST

🕐 **20 MINS**   🍲 **50 MINS**   ✕ **SERVES 6**

PER SERVING:
190 KCAL / 20G CARBS

low-calorie cooking spray
2 carrots, peeled and
   coarsely grated
1 onion, peeled and finely diced
1 courgette, coarsely grated
1 tsp dried thyme
2 tbsp dark soy sauce
2 x 400g tins chickpeas, rinsed
   and drained well
1 tsp garlic granules
60g reduced-fat mature Cheddar,
   grated
30g wholemeal breadcrumbs
sea salt and freshly ground
   black pepper
1 egg, beaten

TO ACCOMPANY *(optional)*
Braised Red Cabbage, page 218
   (+ 87 kcal per serving), steamed
   carrots (+ 32 kcal per serving)

This delicious Vegetable and Chickpea Roast means that vegetarians don't have to miss out on a tasty Sunday lunch! It's packed full of veg to help you get your five a day. The chickpeas add some protein which will keep you feeling full for longer and the seasonings give this dish a lovely umami taste.

Everyday Light ———————

Preheat the oven to 190°C (fan 170°C/gas mark 5). Spray a loaf tin with low-calorie cooking spray and line it with baking parchment.

Spray a large frying pan with low-calorie cooking spray and sauté the carrots, onion and courgette over a medium-high heat. As they cook, they will release some liquid. Keep cooking until this evaporates. It should take 8–9 minutes. Add the thyme and 1 tbsp of the soy sauce and continue cooking for another minute. Remove from the heat.

In a large mixing bowl, mash the chickpeas with a fork or potato masher. You can use a food processor if you wish but be careful not to over process. You want a rough, lumpy texture, not a smooth paste. Add the cooked vegetables and then all the other ingredients, except the salt, pepper and egg, to the bowl. Mix well, and taste. Season with some salt and pepper if you wish. When you are happy with the seasoning, mix in the egg then transfer to the prepared loaf tin, pressing it down firmly. Place in the hot oven for 40 minutes, until it is firm and golden.

Allow to rest for 10 minutes before slicing and serving. (You can also allow to cool and freeze for another day.)

LAMB, ROSEMARY *and* SWEET POTATO PIE

🕐 20 MINS   🍲 1 HOUR 30 MINS   ✕ SERVES 6

(F) (GF) *use GF stock pot*

PER SERVING:
340 KCAL / 40G CARBS

low-calorie cooking spray
1 onion, peeled and chopped
1 garlic clove, peeled and crushed
450g leg of lamb, diced, any
   visible fat removed
300ml beef stock (1 beef stock
   pot dissolved in 300ml boiling
   water)
1 tbsp tomato puree
1 x 400g tin chopped
   tomatoes, drained
2 medium carrots, peeled
   and sliced
150g button mushrooms, sliced
2 sprigs of fresh rosemary
900g sweet potatoes, peeled
   and cut into chunks
1 egg yolk
sea salt and freshly ground
   black pepper
20g reduced-fat Cheddar, grated

TO ACCOMPANY *(optional)*
80g steamed vegetables
   (+ 38 kcal per serving)

Chunks of tender lamb in a rich tomato and rosemary sauce, topped with mashed sweet potato and a sprinkling of cheese. A hearty, warming dish that uses a lean cut of lamb and reduced-fat Cheddar to help keep the calories low. A really satisfying dish that will keep you feeling full for longer, ideal as an alternative to a traditional Sunday roast!

Everyday Light ————————————————

Preheat the oven to 200°C (fan 180°C/gas mark 6).

Spray a medium saucepan with low-calorie cooking spray, place on a medium heat and fry the onion for 5 minutes until softened. Add the garlic and fry for 1–2 minutes. Add the lamb and fry for 1–2 minutes on all sides to seal. Add the stock, tomato puree, drained chopped tomatoes, carrots, mushrooms and rosemary. Cover and simmer on a low heat for 45 minutes–1 hour, or until the lamb is tender. Season to taste.

While the lamb is cooking, cook the sweet potatoes in boiling water for 20 minutes or until tender. Drain the sweet potatoes and mash with the egg yolk until smooth. Season to taste.

When the lamb is tender, place in the bottom of a 18cm x 27cm (roughly 7in x 10½in) ovenproof dish. Spread the mashed sweet potato over the lamb mixture and sprinkle with cheese. Place on a baking tray.

Place in the hot oven and bake for 15–20 minutes until lightly browned.

SWAP THIS: Swap ordinary potatoes for the sweet potatoes or Quorn pieces for the diced lamb.

STEAK DIANE

🕐 **5 MINS** 🍲 **15 MINS** ✕ **SERVES 2**

GF *use Henderson's relish* ↘

PER SERVING:
309 KCAL / 2.7G CARBS

2 x 200g quick-cooking steaks
  (sirloin or rump are ideal)
low-calorie cooking spray
sea salt and freshly ground
  black pepper
75g mushrooms
1 shallot, peeled and finely chopped
1 tsp white wine vinegar
1 tsp Henderson's relish (or
  Worcestershire sauce)
1 tsp Dijon mustard
75ml water
25g light spreadable cheese

TO ACCOMPANY *(optional)*
75g mixed salad (+ 15 kcal
  per serving)

Steak Diane usually features a rich and creamy sauce that's packed full of wine, brandy and cream – not exactly slimming friendly! We've swapped out a few ingredients for low fat and low calorie alternatives so that you can still enjoy this classic dish without all of the extra calories. With an indulgent sauce that's packed full of flavour, this recipe is perfect for a Saturday night in.

Everyday Light ————————————

Spray your steaks on both sides with a little low-calorie cooking spray and season with salt and pepper. Spray a small saucepan with low-calorie cooking spray and sauté the mushrooms and shallot for 5 minutes until soft. Place to one side while you cook your steak.

Place a griddle pan over a medium-high heat. When it is nice and hot, place the steaks in the pan. The cooking time will vary depending on your preference and how thick your steaks are, but a good guide is 2 minutes each side for rare, 3 minutes each side for medium and 4 minutes each side for well done. A rare steak should feel spongy when pressed, a medium steak will have a little resistance and a well-done steak will feel quite firm. When cooked to your liking, remove the steaks from the pan, wrap in foil and allow to rest for 5 minutes while you finish the sauce.

Return the mushrooms and shallot to the heat. Add the white wine vinegar, Henderson's relish and Dijon mustard. Stir, then pour in the water. Allow to simmer for 1 minute, then stir in the soft cheese.

Unwrap the steaks and add any juices to the sauce. Place the steaks on a warmed plate and top with the sauce.

Serve with a crisp mixed salad or your accompaniment of choice.

TIP: Resting your steak allows the juices to be reabsorbed, keeping the meat moist and tender. Try not to skip this step, however hungry you are! It really makes a difference.

FILO FISH PIE

⏱ **15 MINS**   🍲 **1 HOUR 10 MINS**   ✕ **SERVES 4**

A rich fish pie packed with cod, smoked haddock, prawns, leeks and peas. Crispy filo pastry adds crunch, and we've proven you don't need full-fat milk and butter to create a creamy, silky sauce that simply melts in your mouth!

PER SERVING:
318 KCAL /26G CARBS

low-calorie cooking spray
1 onion, peeled and finely chopped
2 leeks, trimmed, washed
 and sliced
1 garlic clove, peeled and crushed
250ml semi-skimmed milk
350g skinless cod fillets, cut into
 large chunks
230g skinless smoked haddock
 fillets, cut into large chunks
2 bay leaves
80g frozen peas
sea salt and freshly ground
 black pepper
175g cooked and peeled
 prawns, drained
1 tbsp cornflour
4 sheets filo pastry, 22cm x 26cm
 (roughly 9in x 10½ in),
 approximately 85g total
1 egg, beaten

TO ACCOMPANY (optional)
80g steamed vegetables
 (+ 38 kcal per serving)

Everyday Light

Preheat the oven to 180°C (fan 160°C/gas mark 4).

Spray a large frying pan (with a lid) with low-calorie cooking spray and place over a medium heat. Add the onion and leeks and fry for 10 minutes, until softened. Add the garlic and fry for 2–3 minutes. Add the milk, cod, haddock, bay leaves, peas and seasoning. Cover and simmer over a low heat for 15 minutes or until the fish is just starting to flake. Don't stir; try to keep the fish in chunks.

Place a colander over a large bowl. Gently tip the contents of the frying pan into the colander to drain off the cooking liquid. Place the drained fish and vegetables in an 18cm x 27cm (roughly 7in x 10½in) ovenproof dish, add the prawns and remove the bay leaves. Set aside.

Place the cooking liquid in the frying pan and place on a medium heat. Mix the cornflour with 1 tbsp of water until smooth. Stir the cornflour mixture into the cooking liquid and simmer for 3–4 minutes until slightly thickened. Season again if needed. Pour the sauce over the fish and vegetables.

Scrunch up each sheet of filo and place on top of the pie. Glaze with the beaten egg.

Place in the oven and cook for 30–35 minutes, until piping hot and golden brown.

SWAP THIS: Swap the cod, haddock and prawns for frozen fish and frozen prawns (defrosted).

TUNA MELT PEPPERS

🕐 **10 MINS**　🍲 **20 MINS**　🍴 **SERVES 4**

GF

PER SERVING:
243 KCAL /21G CARBS

low-calorie cooking spray
1 x 200g tin tuna in spring water
　or brine, drained
125g cooked long-grain rice
½ red onion, peeled and
　finely diced
1 x 100g tin sweetcorn (or cook
　and use frozen)
1 tsp garlic granules
small handful of fresh parsley,
　finely chopped
juice of ½ lemon
120g reduced-fat spreadable
　cheese
80g reduced-fat Cheddar,
　finely grated
sea salt and freshly ground
　black pepper
2 red or orange peppers, sliced
　in half lengthways and the
　seeds removed

TO ACCOMPANY *(optional)*
75g mixed salad (+ 15 kcal
　per serving)

These sweet peppers are stuffed with a cheesy tuna and rice filling and topped with more melted cheese to create a quick, easy and flavourful meal. Great served with a crisp, mixed salad as a light lunch or alongside some potato wedges or extra veg for a more filling meal. We like our peppers to have a bit of bite to them, but if you prefer yours softer, then simply cook the peppers cut side down for 10 minutes before stuffing!

Everyday Light ──────────────────

Preheat the oven to 200°C (fan 180°C/gas mark 6) and spray a baking sheet with low-calorie cooking spray.

Put the tuna, rice, onion, sweetcorn, garlic granules, parsley, lemon juice and cheese spread in a bowl along with half of the grated Cheddar, season with a little salt and pepper and mix well.

Stuff each half-pepper with the tuna mix and place on the baking sheet. Sprinkle with the remaining cheese, and place in the oven for 20 minutes, until the cheese is golden.

Serve with your choice of accompaniment.

▌ **SWAP THIS:** Stuff
large, deseeded tomatoes
instead of peppers.

CORNED BEEF HASH PATTIES

⏱ **15 MINS**   🍲 **40 MINS**   ✕ **SERVES 4**

use GF breadcrumbs ↘

(F) (GF)

PER SERVING:
216 KCAL / 20G CARBS

low-calorie cooking spray
500g potatoes, peeled and cut
  into small chunks
1 onion, peeled and finely diced
1 x 200g tin lean corned beef
15 fresh sage leaves, finely chopped
1 tsp garlic granules
sea salt and freshly ground
  black pepper
1 egg, beaten
60g wholemeal breadcrumbs

TO ACCOMPANY *(optional)*
75g mixed salad (+ 15 kcal
  per serving) and 2 tbsp
  store-bought ketchup
  (+12 kcal per serving)

Crispy on the outside and fluffy on the inside, these Corned Beef Hash Patties are comfort food at its best! We've lightened up this recipe by baking the patties instead of frying them and have used wholemeal breadcrumbs for extra-filling fibre. This is the perfect way to use up leftover mashed potato, as well as any bread that may be going stale!

Everyday Light

Preheat the oven to 200°C (fan 180°C/gas mark 6) and spray a baking sheet with low-calorie cooking spray.

Cook the potatoes in a pan of salted boiling water for about 15 minutes, until a knife slides easily through. Drain well and mash. Leave to one side to cool.

While the potatoes are cooking, spray a frying pan with low-calorie cooking spray and sauté the onion over a medium heat for 3–4 minutes until soft.

Place the corned beef in a large mixing bowl and lightly mash with a fork. Add the potato, sage, onion and garlic granules and mix well. Taste and season with a little salt and pepper.

Shape the potato mix into four even patties. Dip each patty into the beaten egg, then into the breadcrumbs, covering all sides. Place the corned beef hash patties on the baking sheet, spray with low-calorie cooking spray and place in the oven for 15–20 minutes, until the breadcrumbs are golden and crisp.

TIP: This is a great way to use up leftover mashed potato. Save your stale bread to make breadcrumbs. You can make them in advance, pop in a sealable bag and freeze for up to 3 months. Defrost then use as normal.

CREAMY CHICKEN PASTA BAKE

🕐 **10 MINS** 🍲 **45 MINS** ✕ **SERVES 4**

F

PER SERVING:
506 KCAL / 56G CARBS

low-calorie cooking spray
400g diced chicken breast
1 tsp white wine vinegar
1 tsp Henderson's relish (or
  Worcestershire sauce)
200g mushrooms, quartered
1 leek, trimmed and thinly sliced
3 garlic cloves, peeled
  and crushed
400ml chicken stock (2 chicken
  stock cubes dissolved in 400ml
  boiling water)
300g pasta twists
120g reduced-fat spreadable
  cheese
sea salt and freshly ground
  black pepper
80g reduced-fat Cheddar,
  finely grated

TO ACCOMPANY *(optional)*
75g mixed salad (15 kcal
  per serving)

> **TIP:** We've used mushrooms
> in this recipe, but if you have
> a fussy eater in the family, swap
> them out for sweetcorn, peppers
> or any other veg you like.

There is nothing more family friendly than a pasta bake, and we love this one. Creamy chicken, comforting pasta and a cheesy topping. Simple, quick to prepare and utterly delicious!

Special Occasion ─────────────────

Preheat the oven to 200°C (fan 180°C/gas mark 6).

Spray a large frying pan with low-calorie cooking spray and fry the chicken over a high heat for 2 minutes until it is sealed on all sides. Pop on a plate and put to one side.

Lower the heat to medium and add the white wine vinegar and Henderson's relish to the pan and scrape up any browned bits on the bottom. Spray a little more low-calorie cooking spray in the pan, and add the mushrooms and leek. Sauté for 5 minutes until soft. Add the garlic and stock, then return the chicken to the pan. Simmer for 10–15 minutes.

Meanwhile, cook the pasta according to the packet instructions. This will usually take between 9–12 minutes. Drain.

When the chicken is thoroughly cooked, stir in the spreadable cheese. The sauce should be the consistency of single cream. If it is a little thin, increase the heat and reduce for a few minutes until the desired consistency is reached.

Season with a little salt and pepper if needed, then stir in the pasta and pour into an ovenproof dish. Sprinkle with the grated cheese and bake in the oven for 15–20 minutes, until the cheese has melted and is golden. (You can allow to cool and freeze to have another day. Remember to defrost thoroughly before reheating.)

Serve with a crisp mixed salad, if you like.

SUMMER VEGETABLE RISOTTO

🕐 **5 MINS** 🍲 **25 MINS** ✕ **SERVES 4**

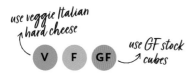

use veggie Italian hard cheese

(V) (F) (GF) → use GF stock cubes

PER SERVING:
353 KCAL / 63G CARBS

low-calorie cooking spray
1 small onion, peeled and
 finely chopped
300g Arborio (risotto) rice
2 tsp white wine vinegar
1 litre vegetable stock (2 vegetable
 stock cubes dissolved in 1 litre
 boiling water)
75g broad beans, fresh or frozen
100g asparagus, cut into 2.5cm
 (1in) pieces
100g Tenderstem broccoli, cut into
 2.5cm (1in) pieces
75g sugar snap peas, halved
juice of 1 lemon
30g Italian hard cheese,
 finely grated (or vegetarian
 hard cheese)
4 spring onions, trimmed and
 thinly sliced
sea salt and freshly ground
 black pepper

A fresh, light meal full of summer flavours and seasonal veggies. It's quick to prepare, and there's no need to constantly stir the rice like you do with a traditional risotto. It's so easy!

Everyday Light ─────────────

Preheat the oven to 180°C (fan 160°C/gas mark 4).

Spray a large casserole pan with low-calorie cooking spray, place over a medium heat, add the onion and sauté for 4–5 minutes until soft. Add the rice and continue cooking, while stirring, for another minute. Stir in the white wine vinegar then pour in the hot stock. Increase the heat and stir until the stock starts to boil. Cover and transfer to the oven. Cook for 15 minutes.

While the rice cooks, place the broad beans, asparagus, broccoli and sugar snap peas in a saucepan of boiling water and simmer for 3 minutes. Drain.

After 15 minutes remove the rice from the oven. The rice should have absorbed almost all the stock. Stir in the lemon juice, grated cheese, spring onions and vegetables, replace the lid and place back in the oven for another 5 minutes.

Taste the rice, add some salt and pepper to taste and serve.

TIP: Use any green vegetables, courgettes, peas, green beans – fresh or frozen – in place of the veg above.

FALAFEL TRAYBAKE

🕐 20 MINS   🍲 40 MINS   ✕ SERVES 4

PER SERVING:
286 KCAL / 51G CARBS

low-calorie cooking spray
500g sweet potatoes, peeled and
  cut into wedges
300g carrots, peeled and cut
  into batons (we've used a mix of
  rainbow heritage carrots and
  normal carrots, but you can use
  all normal carrots if you wish)
2 red onions, peeled and each
  cut into 8 wedges
juice and grated zest of 1 lemon
1 small onion, peeled and
  finely chopped
1 x 400g tin chickpeas, drained
  and rinsed
200g cooked beetroot,
  coarsely grated
½ tsp garlic granules
1 tsp garam masala
a good handful of fresh
  coriander, chopped
sea salt and freshly ground
  black pepper
fresh flat-leaf parsley, to
  serve (optional)

TO ACCOMPANY *(optional)*
75g mixed salad (+ 15 kcal
  per serving)

TIP: Lightly chargrilling
lemon halves for squeezing
over the baked falafel adds
a zingy touch.

We've jazzed up the humble falafel by adding some spices and beetroot to give it a brand new twist. Served with lemony, roasted vegetables, this super simple traybake is low on calories, but still really satisfying. We've used a mixture of normal and rainbow heritage carrots in this recipe, but you can use whichever you prefer.

Everyday Light —————————————

Preheat the oven to 200°C (fan 180°C/gas mark 6).

Spray a large baking sheet (you may need two) with low-calorie cooking spray and scatter the sweet potatoes, carrots and red onion wedges evenly. Squeeze over half the lemon juice, spray with more low-calorie cooking spray and pop in the oven for 15 minutes. While they are cooking, make the falafels.

Spray a frying pan with low-calorie cooking spray, place over a medium heat, add the onion and sauté for 4–5 minutes until soft.

Put the chickpeas in a mixing bowl and mash with a fork. You can use a food processor if you wish, but be careful not to over process. You want a rough mash, rather than a smooth blend.

Wrap the beetroot in a tea towel (one you don't mind staining!) and squeeze out any excess liquid. Add the beetroot to the chickpeas along with the lemon zest, garlic granules, garam masala, sautéed onions and coriander. Taste and add salt and pepper as needed. Divide into twelve equal pieces and roll into balls.

After 15 minutes, remove the vegetables from the oven, toss and squeeze over the remaining lemon juice. Make space for the falafels and place them directly on the tray if you can (they may go soggy if you put them on top of the vegetables). Return to the oven for a further 20–25 minutes, until the falafels are firm and the vegetables are soft.

Serve, garnished with parsley if you like. (The falafels freeze well, so you can cool and pop them in the freezer for another day.)

CHEESY BROCCOLI
STUFFED CHICKEN

🕐 **10 MINS**   🍲 **30 MINS**   ✕ **SERVES 4**

PER SERVING:
196 KCAL / 3.5G CARBS

4 skinless chicken breasts,
   about 120g each
200g broccoli florets, very
   finely chopped
125g light spreadable cheese
½ tsp garlic granules
sea salt and freshly ground
   black pepper

TO ACCOMPANY *(optional)*
75g mixed salad (+ 15 kcal
   per serving)

This dish looks really impressive and tastes absolutely amazing, but it's actually super simple to prepare! The key to achieving a really cheesy filling is to use a very thick, spreadable cheese like GoGo's or Seriously Strong Spreadable Lighter, as thinner types may cause the rolls to lose their shape.

Everyday Light

Preheat the oven to 220°C (fan 200°C/gas mark 7).

Take a chicken breast and cover with a piece of foil or greaseproof paper. Use a rolling pin to bash the meat flat so that it is about 5mm (¼in) thick. Repeat with the rest of the chicken breasts.

In a bowl, add the finely chopped broccoli and cheese spread. Mix to combine. The mixture will be very thick. Split the broccoli–cheese mixture into four and divide amongst the flattened chicken breasts by placing a dollop in the middle and spreading out down the middle of the breast. Roll the chicken up like a tortilla and place in the middle of a piece of foil. Season the top of the chicken with the garlic and salt and pepper to taste. You can also trim the ends with a sharp knife, if you like, to make it look neater. Roll the foil firmly around the chicken and twist the ends like a cracker. Push the ends in slightly so that the chicken is a firm, neat cylinder. Place the chicken 'crackers' onto a baking tray and place in the middle of the hot oven for 30 minutes.

Remove the tray from the oven. Carefully and gently unroll the chicken from the foil – it should now hold its shape. The chicken should be white and cooked throughout. Slice each chicken roll into rounds and serve. (Or you can cool and freeze for another day.)

SWAP THIS: This dish would also work well with leek or cauliflower instead of broccoli.

CHIMICHURRI LAMB CHOPS

⏱ **10 MINS** PLUS 2 HOURS MARINATING TIME 🍲 **15 MINS** ✕ **SERVES 4**

PER SERVING:
235 KCAL / 1.4G CARBS

30g bunch of fresh mint
10g fresh coriander
10g fresh flat-leaf parsley
grated zest and half the juice
 of 1 lemon
2 tbsp red wine vinegar
2 tsp garlic granules
2 tbsp water
½ tsp granulated sweetener
 or sugar
sea salt and freshly ground
 black pepper
8 lamb chops or cutlets, trimmed
 of all visible fat
low-calorie cooking spray

TO ACCOMPANY (optional)
75g mixed salad (+ 15 kcal per
 serving) and 126g (3 medium)
 cooked new potatoes (+ 83 kcal
 per serving)

Chimichurri is a wonderfully herby and tangy sauce originating from Argentina that's typically made with parsley, coriander and oregano mixed with olive oil. We've packed ours with mouth-watering mint to perfectly complement the lamb and kept it light by skipping the oil.

Everyday Light —————————————————

Remove the mint leaves from any tough or woody stalks and place in a food processor or blender along with the coriander and parsley. Blitz on pulse setting until the herbs are finely chopped. Be careful not to over process as you don't want them to turn into a puree. Alternatively, you can finely chop them with a sharp knife. Scrape into a bowl and add the lemon zest and juice, red wine vinegar, garlic granules, water and sweetener. Taste and season with a little salt and pepper if required.

Divide the sauce into two. Take one half and rub liberally onto the lamb chops. Place them in a bowl, cover and refrigerate for between 1–2 hours.

After marinating time, take the lamb chops out of the fridge and allow 15 minutes for them to reach room temperature. Spray a griddle pan or heavy-based frying pan with low-calorie cooking spray and place over a high heat. When the pan is hot, add the lamb chops. Cooking time will vary depending on how thick the chops are and how you like them. We prefer ours medium. You can expect to cook them for between 5 and 7 minutes each side. You may need to cook them in two batches, depending on the size of your pan.

Serve with a little of the remaining sauce drizzled over the top.

TIP: This makes an ideal BBQ dish. The sauce is quite acidic, so don't marinate these overnight – 2 hours is perfect.

CHEESY VEGETABLE PIE

🕐 **20 MINS**   🍲 **1 HOUR 5 MINS**   ✕ **SERVES 6**

use vegetarian hard cheese

(V) ↗

PER SERVING:
585 KCAL / 55G CARBS

FOR THE FILLING
700g sweet potato, peeled and
  cut into cubes
low-calorie cooking spray
3 medium leeks, tops and roots
  removed and cut into 1.5cm
  (just over ½in) thick slices
1 garlic clove, peeled and crushed
½ tsp dried thyme
½ tsp dried oregano
450g ricotta cheese
1 medium egg, beaten
30g Parmesan (or vegetarian hard
  cheese), finely grated
sea salt and freshly ground
  black pepper

FOR THE TOP
6 sheets of filo pastry, each a
  single layer thick, about
  23cm x 26cm (about
  9in x 10½in)
1 small egg, beaten, for glazing

TO ACCOMPANY *(optional)*
80g steamed vegetables
  (+ 38 kcal per serving)

This Cheesy Vegetable Pie is real, hearty comfort food and is packed full of delicious veg. The cheesy filling and topping gives this dish a really indulgent feel, while the use of filo means that the calories are significantly lower than if you were to use another kind of pastry. Perfect when served with lots of steamed veggies!

Special Occasion ─────────────────────

Preheat the oven to 180°C (fan 160°C/gas mark 4).

Place the sweet potatoes in a pan of boiling water. Reduce the heat, cover and simmer for 20–25 minutes or until tender. Drain well and set aside.

While the sweet potatoes are cooking, spray a medium frying pan with low-calorie cooking spray and place over a medium heat. Add the leeks, garlic, thyme and oregano, and fry for 10–15 minutes, or until softened.

Place the sweet potatoes and leek mixture in a large bowl and mix.

In a separate bowl, mix together the ricotta, egg and Parmesan and then add to the vegetable mixture. Stir well to combine and season well with salt and pepper. Tip into an 18cm x 27cm (roughly 7in x 10½in) ovenproof dish and spread out evenly.

Scrunch up a sheet of filo pastry and, starting in one corner, place on top of the vegetable and cheese mixture. Repeat this process until all of the filo pastry covers the top of the pie. Brush the pastry top carefully with beaten egg.

Place on a baking tray and then place in the preheated oven for 30–35 minutes, until the pie is hot right through, and the filo top is golden.

SWAP THIS: Swap the sweet potatoes for ordinary cooked potatoes.

CRUSTLESS
QUICHE LORRAINE

🕐 **10 MINS** 🍲 **22 MINS** 🍴 **SERVES 4**

PER SERVING:
336 KCAL / 6.2G CARBS

4 smoked bacon medallions, all
   visible fat removed
1 large onion, peeled
low-calorie cooking spray
6 large eggs
4 tbsp plain quark
sea salt and freshly ground
   black pepper
160g reduced-fat Cheddar, grated

TO ACCOMPANY *(optional)*
75g mixed salad (+ 15 kcal
   per serving)

We think this quiche has way more flavour than a
shop-bought version and it's so quick and easy to
make. The classic version features onion and bacon,
but you could really add any of your favourite
vegetables. Why not try mushrooms, peppers or
spinach? Serve this dish hot or cold and you could
even pop it into a lunch box for a quick picnic lunch!

Everyday Light ───────────────────────

Preheat the oven to 180°C (fan 160°C/gas mark 4). Chop the
bacon into thin strips and finely dice the onion.

Spray a large frying pan with low-calorie cooking spray and place
over a medium heat. Add the bacon strips and diced onion and
cook until the bacon has coloured and the onion is soft. Set aside
to cool slightly.

Place the eggs into a large bowl and whisk. Add the quark and
continue to whisk until the quark is fully combined – there should
be no lumps at all. Season well with salt and pepper. Stir in
half of the cheese and the bacon-and-onion mix. Spray a
24cm (9½in) flan dish with low-calorie cooking spray and pour in
the egg mixture. Make sure that there is an even distribution of
bacon and onion. Top with the remaining cheese and cook for
20 minutes until golden. If using a dish with a smaller diameter
(therefore resulting in a deeper quiche), then it may need an
extra 5–6 minutes in the oven.

Serve hot or leave to cool and eat cold (or you can pop it in the
freezer to have another time).

CHICKEN KIEVS

🕐 **10 MINS** 🍲 **30 MINS** ✕ **SERVES 4**

use GF bread and stock pots ↗

PER SERVING:
268 KCAL / 9.9G CARBS

3 garlic cloves
handful of fresh parsley
2 vegetable stock pots
2 tsp water
20g reduced-fat spread
sea salt and finely ground
  black pepper
60g wholemeal bread
4 chicken breasts (skin and
  visible fat removed)
2 eggs
low-calorie cooking spray
lemon wedges, to serve

TO ACCOMPANY *(optional)*
80g steamed vegetables
  (+ 38 kcal per serving)
Lemon and Garlic Asparagus,
  page 200 (+ 40 kcal per serving)
Lyonnaise Potatoes, page 204
  (+ 255 kcal per serving – this will
  turn it into a Special Occasion
  recipe)

Our slimming-friendly take on this classic dish is so delicious that you'd never guess it was low on calories! We've used garlic and parsley to flavour these kievs, but you can easily adapt the dish to your tastes by replacing the garlic with some chilli, or swapping the parsley for some chives instead – get experimenting!

Weekly Indulgence

Preheat the oven to 190°C (fan 170°C/gas mark 5) and line a baking tray with greaseproof paper.

Place the garlic, parsley, vegetable stock pots, water and reduced-fat spread into a mini electric chopper. Whizz until the garlic and parsley are chopped quite finely, but still retain some texture. Season with salt and pepper. Place into a dish and chill for 15 minutes.

Using the mini electric chopper again, whizz the bread into fine breadcrumbs.

With a very sharp knife, cut a pocket into the chicken – place the knife into one end, being careful not to cut through to the outside.

Once the garlic mixture has chilled, spoon evenly into the pocket in the chicken breasts, filling as much as possible. Pin closed with a cocktail stick.

Beat the eggs and place into a shallow dish. Place the breadcrumbs into a separate shallow dish. Dip each chicken breast into the egg and then lightly cover with breadcrumbs. Place each crumbed chicken breast onto the baking tray, spray with low-calorie cooking spray and cook for 30 minutes until golden and crisp. (At this point you could cool and freeze for another day, remembering to defrost thoroughly before reheating.)

Serve with a wedge of lemon and your choice of accompaniment!

TOAD-IN-THE-HOLE

🕐 **5 MINS**   🍲 **35 MINS**   ✕ **SERVES 3**

(F)

PER SERVING:
355 KCAL / 37G CARBS

6 reduced-fat pork sausages
2 eggs
30g plain flour
75ml skimmed milk
sea salt and freshly ground
    black pepper
low-calorie cooking spray

FOR THE GRAVY
1 medium carrot, diced
½ onion, peeled and diced
1 medium potato, peeled
    and diced
600ml water
2 chicken or beef stock pots
4 drops of gravy browning
    (or to taste)

TO ACCOMPANY *(optional)*
80g steamed vegetables
    (+ 38 kcal per serving)

This dish was a rare Sunday treat during the colder months when we were kids and it always had us begging for more! Toad-in-the-Hole is comfort food at its best and it's really cheap and easy to make as well. If you want to add a twist to it, then you could add some onions or use spicy sausages – you could even add some red onion marmalade, if you like!

Everyday Light ───────────────────

Preheat the oven to 220°C (fan 200°C/gas mark 7).

Bake the sausages on an oven tray for 10 minutes until they are not quite cooked and only slightly browned.

Meanwhile, make the batter. In a bowl whisk the eggs, flour, milk and salt until smooth. Season and set aside in the fridge.

Now get started on the gravy. Put the carrot, onion and potato in a saucepan with the water. Bring to the boil then simmer for about 25 minutes, or until the vegetables are cooked.

Remove the sausages from the oven, set aside on a plate, then turn the oven up to 230°C (fan 210°C/gas mark 7–8). Spray the oven tray with a decent amount of low-calorie cooking spray and put it in the oven until it starts to foam (about 5 minutes). Place the sausages in the hot tray, give the batter a quick stir and pour it into the tray with the sausages. Bake in the oven for 10 minutes, then turn the oven down to just under 220°C (fan 200°C/gas mark 7) and cook for another 5–10 minutes (you can open the oven door to have a peek after about 15 minutes).

Stir the stock pots and gravy browning into the vegetables until dissolved, then blitz with a hand blender until smooth.

When the batter is risen, nicely browned and crisp, remove from the oven and serve with the gravy. (Or you can cool and freeze to have another day. Defrost thoroughly before reheating.)

SNACKS
and
SIDES

~

CHAPTER 6

Super
QUICK

LEMON *and* GARLIC ASPARAGUS

⏱ **2 MINS**   🍲 **10 MINS**   ✕ **SERVES 4**

PER SERVING:
40 KCAL / 3.1G CARBS

500g asparagus
juice of 1 lemon
1 tsp garlic granules
sea salt and freshly ground
   black pepper

This simple, but tasty veggie side dish works perfectly with pretty much any meal, but especially fish or chicken! Asparagus is a delicious veg that doesn't need much adding to it, so we've just enhanced the natural flavour with some lemon juice and garlic. This is a great way to get one of your five a day and will help to leave you feeling full for longer.

Everyday Light

Snap off the bottom of the asparagus to remove the woody ends. Discard the ends. If you are using asparagus tips, then you won't need to do this part.

In a small frying pan, add the asparagus and the lemon juice and place over a medium heat. Sprinkle over the garlic granules and season with salt and pepper to taste.

Cook for about 10 minutes until the asparagus is tender (it should have softened but still have some bite). This could take a little more or less time depending on how thick the asparagus is.

Serve as a side to your favourite dish.

SWAP THIS: Swap the fresh lemon juice for 2 tbsp concentrated lemon juice, or use 1 crushed fresh garlic clove (peeled first) instead of the garlic granules.

BOMBAY POTATOES

🕐 **10 MINS** 🍲 **25 MINS** ✗ **SERVES 4**

PER SERVING:
167 KCAL / 32G CARBS

700g new potatoes, scrubbed
   and halved
low-calorie cooking spray
1 onion, peeled and finely diced
20g piece of root ginger, peeled
   and chopped
2 garlic cloves, peeled and
   chopped
1 green chilli, deseeded and
   finely chopped
2 tsp garam masala
1 tsp ground cumin
½ tbsp ground coriander
½ tsp ground turmeric
1 x 160g tin chopped tomatoes
sea salt and freshly ground
   black pepper
small bunch of fresh coriander,
   chopped, to serve

A classic accompaniment to any Indian dish, our take on Bombay Potatoes is big on flavour, but low on calories. The combination of potatoes, herbs, spices and juicy tomatoes means that this dish works really well when served alongside pretty much any curry. These Bombay Potatoes are also perfect for reheating for a light lunch the next day!

Everyday Light ———————————————

Put the potatoes in a large saucepan. Cover with salted cold water and bring to the boil. Once the water is boiling, reduce the heat and simmer for 8–10 minutes. When the potatoes are tender, drain and let air dry.

While the potatoes are cooking, spray a frying pan with low-calorie cooking spray and then fry the onions, ginger, garlic and chilli for 10–15 minutes. Add the garam masala, cumin, coriander and turmeric to the pan and fry for a further 2 minutes, stirring so that nothing burns. Add the tinned tomatoes and cooked potatoes. Mix well and cook for a further 5 minutes until the potatoes are hot all the way through.

Season to taste with salt and pepper. Sprinkle with chopped coriander and serve. (You can also choose to reheat later, or you can cool and freeze for another day.)

LYONNAISE POTATOES

⏱ **15 MINS**　🍲 **45 MINS**　✕ **SERVES 4**

(V) (F) (GF) *use GF stock cubes* ↗

PER SERVING:
255 KCAL / 51G CARBS

1kg potatoes, peeled and cut
　into 5mm (¼in) slices
2 chicken or vegetable
　stock cubes
low-calorie cooking spray
2 onions, peeled and thinly sliced
sea salt and freshly ground
　black pepper

Typically cooked in a pan in lashings of butter, traditional Lyonnaise potatoes are time-consuming and packed full of calories. Not only have we reduced the calories in our version, but we've also reduced the amount of effort too. We like pairing them with meat, particularly our Pork and Apple Traybake (page 154) and Viking Pork (page 156).

Weekly Indulgence

Preheat the oven to 210°C (fan 190°C/gas mark 7).

Put the potato slices in a saucepan and just cover with cold water. Crumble the stock cubes straight into the pan, turn the heat up high and bring to the boil.

Meanwhile, spray a medium frying pan with low-calorie cooking spray and sauté the onions over a medium-high heat until golden brown – this should take around 10 minutes. Season the onions with a little salt and pepper.

When the potatoes have come to the boil, reduce the heat and simmer for 5 minutes. Reserve 60ml of the cooking liquid and drain.

Spray an ovenproof dish with low-calorie cooking spray and spread half of the potatoes on the bottom. Scatter the onions evenly over the potato layer, then arrange the remaining potatoes on top. Pour the reserved stock over, season the potatoes with salt and freshly ground black pepper, then spray with low-calorie cooking spray.

Place in the oven and cook for 30 minutes until the top is golden and the potatoes are soft enough to slide a knife easily through.

Serve. (You can also cool and freeze to have another day.)

TIP: Don't discard the cooking liquid as it also makes a tasty base for soup or gravy.

COBB SALAD

🕐 **15 MINS** 🍲 **10 MINS** 🍴 **SERVES 4**

PER SERVING:
368 KCAL /11G CARBS

FOR THE SALAD
4 eggs
low-calorie cooking spray
240g chicken breast (skin and
   visible fat removed), diced
4 smoked bacon medallions, diced
4 tomatoes, diced
1 x 200g tin sweetcorn, drained
1 medium avocado, peeled and
   thinly sliced
1 small red onion, peeled and
   thinly sliced
sea salt and freshly ground
   black pepper
1 small head of iceberg lettuce,
   washed and roughly diced

FOR THE DRESSING
35g blue cheese
3 tbsp fat-free Greek or
   natural yoghurt
1 tsp white wine vinegar
½ tsp mustard powder
sea salt and freshly ground
   black pepper

An American favourite since the 1930s, this hearty salad is packed full of tasty meat and veggies, with a tangy dressing. We've used plenty of chicken, bacon and egg to keep you full for longer, but this dish is so versatile you can use your own favourite ingredients and dressings too. It makes an ideal lunch or light dinner.

Everyday Light ─────────────

Put the eggs in a medium saucepan. Cover with water and bring to the boil. Once the water is bubbling cook for 6 minutes. Remove the eggs from the pan with a slotted spoon and leave to cool in a bowl of cold water. Once the eggs are cooled peel them carefully. You can do this under a running tap to make it easier. Slice into quarters and set aside.

While the eggs are cooking, spray a large frying pan with low-calorie cooking spray and add the chicken and bacon. Cook over a medium heat for 7–10 minutes, stirring occasionally, until the chicken is white throughout.

While the other ingredients are cooking, make the dressing. Crumble the blue cheese into a small bowl. Mix it together with the yoghurt, vinegar and mustard powder. If you find it is too thick, add a little splash of water and season with salt and pepper to taste. Set aside.

To assemble the salad, you can either mix all the ingredients together in a serving bowl or place the lettuce in the bottom of a bowl and arrange the remaining ingredients on top. Serve with a drizzle of dressing.

SWAP THIS: Swap the chicken for turkey or a 'chicken' veggie substitute, swap the bacon for a veggie alternative. Veggies and the avocado can be left out or swapped by preference.

TIP: If there is an ingredient you don't have or don't like, just leave it out or swap it for something you do!

'I don't feel like I'm eating low-calorie food. I enjoy my food more now than when I wasn't trying to cut down on calories!'

HANNAH

CAULIFLOWER CHEESE *and* POTATO MASH

🕐 **15 MINS**   🍲 **30 MINS**   ✗ **SERVES 4**

PER SERVING:
248 KCAL / 32G CARBS

1 medium cauliflower, cut
   into florets
low-calorie cooking spray
sea salt and freshly ground
   black pepper
3 large potatoes, about 200g
   each, peeled and cut into large
   chunks
5g fresh parsley, chopped
120g reduced-fat Cheddar, grated

Everyone knows that cheese makes everything better! This Cauliflower Cheese and Potato Mash has less carbs than traditional mashed potatoes, but it's still super hearty and full of flavour. A perfect accompaniment to most meals, and really easy to prepare, we think that it works particularly well when served as part of a roast dinner or with our Mushroom Bourguignon on page 139.

Weekly Indulgence ─────────────

Preheat the oven to 220°C (fan 200°C/gas mark 7).

Place the cauliflower florets onto a baking tray and spray with low-calorie cooking spray. Sprinkle with salt and pepper and cook for 30 minutes until golden brown and softened.

While the cauliflower is cooking, place the potatoes into a pan of salted cold water and bring to the boil. Reduce the heat and simmer for 25–30 minutes until soft, then drain.

When both the cauliflower and potatoes are cooked, mash together until smooth. Add the parsley and grated cheese, and mix well. Season with salt and pepper if needed and serve. (Or you can cool and freeze for later.)

SWAP THIS: Use frozen cauliflower instead of fresh.

Super
EASY

LIME *and* COCONUT JASMINE RICE

🕐 **5 MINS**　　🗑 **18 MINS**　　✕ **SERVES 4**

VE　**F**　**GF**

PER SERVING:
234 KCAL / 50G CARBS

FOR THE RICE
240g jasmine rice
400ml dairy-free coconut
　milk alternative
100ml water
2 tsp granulated sweetener
sea salt and freshly ground
　black pepper
grated zest and juice of 1 lime

FOR THE GARNISH
1 lime, cut into quarters
2g fresh coriander, chopped

This Lime and Coconut Jasmine Rice recipe is our healthy twist on a fragrant and tangy Thai rice dish. We've swapped the high-fat canned coconut milk for a dairy-free alternative which promises all of the flavour without the calories! Why not try it with our Teriyaki Chicken on page 48.

Weekly Indulgence ───────────

Place the rice in a sieve and rinse thoroughly under cold running water, until the water runs clear.

In a medium saucepan bring the coconut milk alternative, water and sweetener to the boil, add the rice, a pinch of salt, and cover, then turn the heat to low. Allow to simmer for 15 minutes until all of the liquid has been absorbed. Test the rice. If it is too firm, you can add a little more water and continue to cook until it becomes tender. Remove from the heat and stir in the lime juice and zest. Season with pepper to taste. (At this point you could cool and freeze for another day.)

Serve garnished with a wedge of lime and chopped coriander.

BOMBAY CHICKPEAS

🕐 **5 MINS**   🗑 **40 MINS**   ✕ **SERVES 4**

PER SERVING:
78 KCAL / 9.2G CARBS

1 x 400g tin chickpeas, drained
  and rinsed
low-calorie cooking spray
1 tsp garam masala
1 tsp onion salt
½ tsp garlic granules

The humble chickpea is not just for hummus! Oven roasted instead of fried, they make a great low-calorie treat and are packed with protein to help keep hunger at bay. Perfect for movie-night snacking!

Everyday Light ─────────────────────

Preheat the oven to 200°C (fan 180°C/gas mark 6).

Spread the chickpeas out on a clean tea towel or absorbent cloth. Place another clean towel on top and roll gently around for a couple of minutes to dry the chickpeas. This will also remove some shells, so pick them out.

Line a baking sheet with baking parchment and scatter the chickpeas on it. Spray with low-calorie cooking spray and spread out evenly in a thin layer. You want plenty of space between the chickpeas to make sure they crisp up. Place in the oven for 25 minutes, giving the tray a shake halfway through. Now mix the garam masala, onion salt and garlic granules in a bowl.

After 25 minutes, remove the chickpeas from the oven and give them another spray with low-calorie cooking spray. Tip into the bowl and mix with the spices until well coated. Scatter back onto the baking sheet and return to the oven for another 10–15 minutes until crisp.

Serve either straight from the oven while warm, or cool and store in an airtight jar for later.

SWAP THIS:
Swap the garam masala for curry powder.

TIP: These can also be cooked in an air fryer. Spray with low-calorie cooking spray and cook in the air fryer for 12 minutes. Remove, spray with a little more low-calorie cooking spray, then toss in the spices and return to the air fryer for 5 more minutes, or until crisp. If you like things spicy, add some chilli powder or cayenne pepper to the spice mix.

SIMPLE NAAN BREAD

⏱ **10 MINS** PLUS 45 MINS PROVING   🍲 **8 MINS**   ✕ **SERVES 4**

PER SERVING:
278 KCAL / 52G CARBS

250g white self-raising flour
1 tsp caster sugar
½ tsp salt
½ tsp baking powder
250g fat-free natural yoghurt
10g reduced-fat spread,
   plus a little extra for greasing

Naan bread has been firmly off the menu for many of us as it's usually so high in calories. Readily available ingredients transform this simple naan bread that tastes wonderful; have one with a curry and it's a real treat. These are so quick and easy to make and such a great addition to many dishes that they will be enjoyed by everyone!

Weekly Indulgence ————————————

Sift the flour, sugar, salt and baking powder into a large bowl. Make a well in the centre and add the yoghurt. Using your fingertips, gradually draw the flour into the yoghurt, mixing to form a ball of soft dough.

Place the dough on a lightly floured surface and knead well for 5 minutes until the dough forms a smooth ball. Place the dough in a large lightly greased bowl and cover with cling film.

Place in a warm place for approximately 45 minutes until the dough has increased slightly in size and feels slightly puffy when pressed. Preheat the oven to 220°C (fan 200°C/gas mark 7).

Turn the dough out onto a lightly floured surface and, using a sharp knife, cut into four equal pieces. If the dough is sticky, dust with a little more flour. Form into four oval-shaped balls, then roll out into ovals approximately 11cm x 22cm (roughly 4½in x 9in).

Place the naan bread on two lightly greased baking trays and prick with a fork. Bake in the preheated oven for 8 minutes or until lightly golden and puffy.

Remove from the baking trays and place on a cooling rack.

Place the reduced-fat spread in a small saucepan over a very low heat. Heat until just melted, then use to brush over the naan breads. Serve at once, while still warm. (You can also cool your naan bread and freeze for later. Defrost before reheating.)

BRAISED RED CABBAGE

🕐 **10 MINS** 🍲 **1 HOUR** ✕ **SERVES 6**

VE **F** **GF**

PER SERVING:
87 KCAL / 14G CARBS

low-calorie cooking spray
1 red onion, peeled and chopped
1 red cabbage, about 1kg, cut into
    5mm (¼in) shreds
1 apple, peeled and cut into
    1cm (½in) dice
grated zest and juice of 1 orange
200ml water
3 tbsp balsamic vinegar
1 tsp golden granulated
    sweetener or sugar
1 cinnamon stick
sea salt and freshly ground
    black pepper

The perfect accompaniment to any roast dinner, the tangy, fruity taste of this Braised Red Cabbage works exceptionally well with pork, and our Vegetable and Chickpea Roast on page 168. The warming hint of cinnamon means that this dish would also be the perfect addition to your Christmas dinner. You can even make it ahead of time and store it covered in the fridge for 2–3 days – perfect if you want to get on top of your prep!

Everyday Light ———————————————

Spray a large casserole pan with low-calorie cooking spray, place over a medium heat, add the onion and sauté for 3–4 minutes until it begins to soften.

Add the remaining ingredients to the pan, except the salt and pepper, stir well and bring to a simmer. Turn the heat down low, cover and allow to simmer gently for 50 minutes, stirring occasionally.

After 50 minutes, remove the lid and take out the cinnamon stick. If there is a lot of liquid remaining, increase the heat and stir until most of it has evaporated. Season with salt and pepper to taste and serve. (Or you can cool and freeze to have another day.)

COLESLAW

🕐 **15 MINS** 🍲 **NO COOK** ✕ **SERVES 6**

PER SERVING:
80 KCAL / 12G CARBS

½ white cabbage
(about 450g), shredded
1 onion (or 1 small red and 1 small
brown onion), peeled and sliced
3 medium carrots, peeled
and grated
100g fat-free natural yoghurt
32g quark
½ tsp mustard powder
1 tbsp lemon juice
sea salt and freshly ground
black pepper

Our slimming-friendly version of this classic side dish is not only lower in calories, but also lower in fat as well! The perfect accompaniment to any barbecue, salad, quiche, burger, or even a jacket potato, this dish is so tasty that you'd never guess it was low on calories. This recipe makes a big batch of coleslaw which is perfect for buffets and barbecues!

Everyday Light ————————————————

Mix the cabbage, onion and carrots together.

In another bowl, mix together the yoghurt, quark, mustard powder and lemon juice. Beat well to remove any lumps.

Combine the veg and the yoghurt mix, then season with salt and pepper to taste. Serve.

ORZO PRIMAVERA PASTA SALAD

🕐 **10 MINS**   🍲 **10 MINS**   ✕ **SERVES 4**

use GF orzo

VE   **GF**

PER SERVING:
213 KCAL / 41G CARBS

200g orzo
1 tsp ground turmeric
1 tbsp red wine vinegar
½ tsp dried oregano
½ tbsp lemon juice
1 tbsp pickled vegetable juice
  (the pickling liquid from a jar
  of pickles)
1 tbsp water
sea salt and freshly ground
  black pepper
½ red onion, peeled
¼ red pepper, deseeded
¼ green pepper, deseeded
1 tbsp fresh parsley, plus extra
  to serve (optional)
14 cherry tomatoes (we've used
  a selection pack with four
  different types)

If you've never heard of orzo before, it may look like rice, but it's actually a type of pasta! It makes a great alternative to fusilli or penne and is perfect for this dish. Packed full of loads of tasty veg, this pasta salad is great when served as part of a barbecue, or as an accompaniment to a main meal, such as our Chicken Shashlik on page 70. It's also delicious when served as a light lunch!

Weekly Indulgence ———————————————

Place the orzo into a decent-sized pan, then add the turmeric. Cover with plenty of boiling, salted water, stir and bring to the boil. Turn the heat down and simmer. Cook the orzo according to the packet instructions – it usually takes 8–10 minutes.

Meanwhile, make the dressing by mixing the red wine vinegar, oregano, lemon juice, pickled veg juice, water and seasoning together well. Set aside.

Finely chop the onion, peppers and parsley, and cut the tomatoes in half.

Remove the orzo from the heat, then plunge it into cold water to cool it down and stop it from overcooking and clumping together. Drain it well.

Tip all of the ingredients into a large bowl, check the seasoning and add some more salt and pepper if necessary. Mix well and serve sprinkled with some more chopped fresh parsley if you wish.

BEETROOT *and* MINT HUMMUS

Super **QUICK**

🕐 **5 MINS**　🍲 **NO COOK**　✕ **SERVES 2**

PER SERVING:
156 KCAL / 22G CARBS

1 x 400g tin butter beans, drained
1 cooked beetroot
handful of fresh mint, chopped
juice of 1 lemon
2 tsp white wine vinegar
sea salt

TO ACCOMPANY *(optional)*
vegetable crudités – 6 baby
  carrots, peeled (+ 39 kcal per
  serving), ¼ cucumber (+ 24 kcal
  per serving), ½ red pepper
  (+ 11 kcal per serving), handful
  of Tenderstem broccoli (+ 23 kcal
  per serving), 6 baby corn
  (+ 30 kcal per serving). Cut
  the vegetables lengthways on
  a diagonal, to the length of
  your choice.

Our slimming-friendly take on a dip we tried at a summer barbecue, this recipe couldn't be easier to make. Just throw all of the ingredients together and blend – that's it! You can really serve this dip with anything that you like, but we love it with some crunchy vegetable crudités. Our top tip is to cut your cucumber, carrots and celery lengthways and on a diagonal so that you can scoop up as much hummus as possible!

Weekly Indulgence ————————————

Tip all of the ingredients into a blender/food processor and blitz. You can also pop them into a bowl and attack with a stick blender! Season to taste and serve with your favourite crudités.

SWAP THIS: If you can't get hold of fresh mint, then you can also use 3 tsp of mint sauce instead. You'll need to double check the nutritional values, though, as these can vary.

TIP: You could use large pickled beetroot if you can't get hold of a ready-cooked one. Make sure that you leave out the white wine vinegar if you do this, as you probably won't need it!

Sweet
treats

~

CHAPTER 7

BAILEYS CHOCOLATE CHEESECAKE POTS

🕐 **10 MINS** PLUS 2 HOURS CHILLING   🍲 **NO COOK**   ✕ **SERVES 10**

 V GF *use GF cookies* ↗

PER SERVING:
108 KCAL / 5.8G CARBS

250g ricotta cheese
400g fat-free Greek yoghurt
150g extra-light cream cheese
60ml Baileys Irish Cream
4 tbsp granulated sweetener
1 tsp vanilla extract
1½ sachets of vegetarian gelatine
2 small double-chocolate cookies,
   lightly crushed

Little pots of delectably creamy Baileys-flavoured cheesecake topped with crushed double-chocolate cookies. These cheesecakes are light and creamy while low in fat, and so simple to make with just a few ingredients. A tasty treat for dessert, strictly for the grown-ups!

Everyday Light 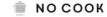 ─────────────

Place the ricotta, yoghurt, cream cheese, Baileys, sweetener and vanilla extract in a mixing bowl and mix until smooth.

Make up gelatine according to the packet instructions and whisk into the cheesecake mix until fully incorporated. Pour the mix equally into ten 100ml ramekin dishes and refrigerate for at least 2 hours.

When set, top with crushed cookies and serve.

TIP: You can make 1 large cheesecake by pouring all of the mixture into one large dish and letting it set in the fridge. Spoon out individual portions when ready to serve.

CHOCOLATE TARTS

⏱ **20 MINS** 🍲 **30 MINS** ✕ **SERVES 12**

PER SERVING:
74 KCAL / 6.3G CARBS

low-calorie cooking spray
1 sheet of light, ready-rolled
  puff pastry
100ml milk
30g dark chocolate, grated
1 large egg
1 egg yolk
2 tbsp granulated brown
  sweetener
½ tsp icing sugar

Chocolate lovers, rejoice! Our slimming-friendly recipe means that Chocolate Tarts are back on the menu! These little treats are big enough to satisfy your sweet tooth and combine crisp, flaky pastry with a creamy, indulgent chocolate filling. Enjoy them served warm as a dessert, or cold alongside a cuppa or a coffee for an afternoon snack.

Everyday Light

Preheat the oven to 180°C (fan 160°C/gas mark 4).

Spray the moulds of a shallow muffin tray with low-calorie cooking spray. Cut out twelve circles of pastry with a 10cm (4in) pastry cutter. Line each mould of the muffin tray with a pastry circle, pressing carefully into the sides.

Heat the milk in a microwave in a microwaveable jug. Don't boil it, it just needs to be warm enough to melt the chocolate (if you make your milk too hot, then this may cause your eggs to scramble!). Stir the chocolate into the milk and allow it to melt.

Beat together the egg, egg yolk and sweetener in a bowl. When it is well combined, stir in the chocolate milk. Pour the chocolate custard into the pastry cases, and place in the oven for 20–25 minutes, until the pastry is golden, and the custard is set.

Dust with the icing sugar and serve either hot or cold.

Super
EASY

SALTED CARAMEL RICE KRISPIE BARS

🕐 **5 MINS** PLUS 2 HOURS CHILLING   🥘 **10 MINS**   ✕ **SERVES 8**

V

PER SERVING:
115 KCAL /20G CARBS

low-calorie cooking spray
135g sugar-free chewy caramels
3 tbsp semi-skimmed milk
½ tsp sea salt
80g puffed rice cereal

Sweet and salty caramel krispie bars, ideal for an indulgent afternoon treat. These delicious no-bake krispie bars are made using melted sugar-free chewy caramels, an ingenious alternative to traditional caramel. The real challenge is having just one!

Everyday Light

Spray an 18cm (7in) square cake tin with a little low-calorie cooking spray and use to grease the tin. Line the tin with greaseproof paper.

Place the caramels, milk and ¼ tsp of salt in a small saucepan and place over a low heat, stirring continuously for 7–10 minutes until just melted. Remove from the heat immediately.

Place the puffed rice cereal in a large bowl and pour in the caramel mixture. Stir until well combined and tip into the prepared tin. Spread the mixture out evenly and press down slightly. Sprinkle with the remaining ¼ tsp of salt.

Chill for a minimum of 2 hours, but preferably overnight to give a firmer result. Remove from the tin and cut into eight bars.

SWEET POTATO BROWNIES

🕐 **10 MINS**   🍲 **40 MINS**   ✕ **SERVES 16**

PER SERVING:
96 KCAL / 8.8G CARBS

FOR THE BROWNIES
200g sweet potatoes, peeled
  and cut into small chunks
100g reduced-fat spread, plus
  a little extra for greasing
125g brown granulated sweetener
100g plain flour
2 medium eggs
½ tsp vanilla extract
¼ tsp baking powder
50g cocoa powder

FOR THE TOPPING
1½ tbsp maple syrup
1 tbsp cocoa powder

Moist and fudgy chocolate squares drizzled with a little chocolate sauce made with a surprising secret ingredient! We've used a mixture of maple syrup and cocoa powder to give a lower-calorie alternative to chocolate. It is just like the real thing and just as delicious!

Everyday Light ———————————————————

Preheat the oven to 180°C (fan 160°C/gas mark 4). Grease and line an 18cm x 18cm (7in x 7in) square cake tin with greaseproof paper.

Place the sweet potatoes in a pan of boiling water. Lower the heat and simmer, covered, for 10–15 minutes until tender. Drain and mash. Leave to cool completely.

When the sweet potatoes are cool, place them in a mixing bowl along with all the other brownie ingredients. Using an electric hand whisk, beat together for 2–3 minutes. Tip into the prepared tin and spread out, levelling the surface with a knife. Place in the preheated oven and bake for 25 minutes. Remove from the oven and leave in the tin to cool completely.

In a small bowl, mix the maple syrup with the cocoa powder until smooth.

Remove the brownies and greaseproof paper from the tin, drizzle with the chocolate topping and cut into sixteen squares. Remove carefully from the greaseproof paper. (You can also choose to freeze the brownies for another day.)

PINEAPPLE *with* LIME *and* CINNAMON

🕐 **5 MINS** 🍲 **30 MINS** ✕ **SERVES 4**

PER SERVING:
91 KCAL /18G CARBS

juice of 2 limes, made up to
 125ml with water
finely grated zest of 2 limes
2 tsp brown granulated sweetener
½ tsp ground cinnamon
4 x 1cm (½in) thick slices
 fresh ripe pineapple, cored
 and skin removed
lime wedges, to serve

TO ACCOMPANY *(optional)*
50g fat-free Greek yoghurt
 (+ 29 kcal per serving)

A simple, sweet and sticky dish with zesty citrus flavours and fresh fruit, inspired by a classic Brazilian dessert. We can't promise the Brazilian weather, but we can promise a sweet, tropical treat! Substituting the traditional brown sugar with a brown sugar sweetener keeps the calories low.

Everyday Light ────────────────

Mix together the lime juice, water, lime zest, sweetener and cinnamon in a small bowl. Pour into a medium ovenproof frying pan and add the pineapple slices. Turn the pineapple slices a few times to coat in the mixture. Place over a high heat and bring to a boil.

Cover and reduce the heat to medium. Simmer for 20–25 minutes, turning occasionally, until tender and the liquid has reduced down to form a sticky coating. Preheat the grill to high.

Take the pan off the heat and put it under the grill to brown lightly. Serve with lime wedges and some Greek yoghurt, if you like.

SWAP THIS: Use tinned pineapple instead of fresh pineapple (reduce the cooking time).

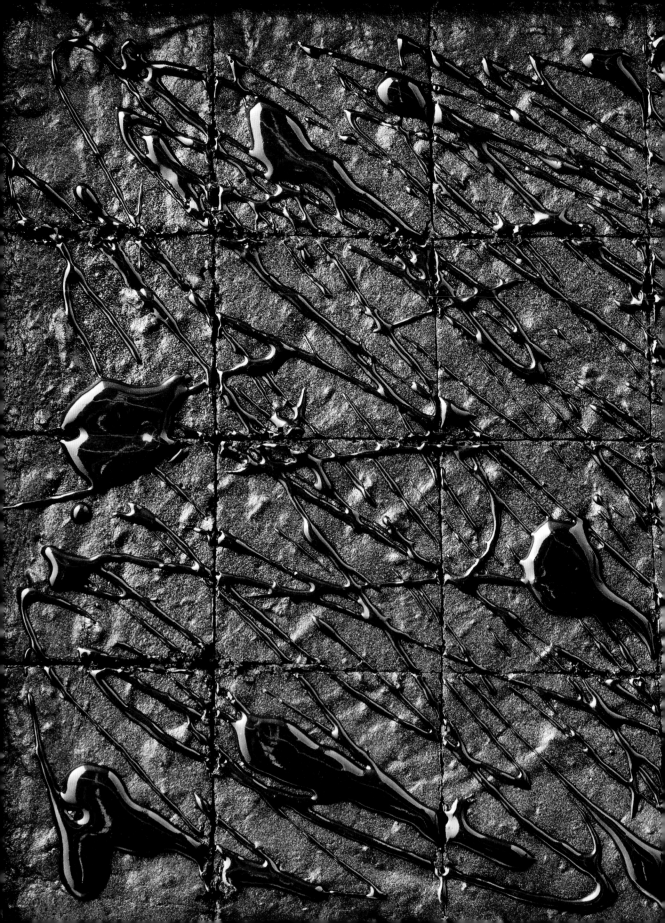

'No matter what
you have in your fridge
and cupboards, there
will be a tasty and
healthy recipe from
Pinch of Nom.'

~

DEB

BLUEBERRY, GIN *and* BANANA ICE CREAM

🕐 **10 MINS** PLUS MARINATING AND FREEZING TIME   🗑 **NO COOK**   ✕ **SERVES 6**

PER SERVING:
98 KCAL /18G CARBS

400g frozen blueberries
2 tbsp granulated sweetener
25ml gin
4 medium bananas, peeled and
  cut in half

This ice cream will knock your socks off! Although it's dairy free and fat free, it's also super creamy and tastes just like the full-fat stuff. The even better news is that you only need four ingredients to whip it up and it packs a boozy punch too. It's the perfect choice for when you fancy a naughty, grown-up dessert without all of those pesky extra calories!

Everyday Light

Take 50g of the blueberries and put them in a small bowl with the sweetener and the gin. Cover and leave the bowl in the fridge overnight – the longer the blueberries soak in the gin, the more boozy they'll be.

Place the banana halves into a lidded freezer-proof container and freeze them overnight.

The next day, take the frozen bananas and the remaining 350g of frozen blueberries out of the freezer. Place them into a food processor (or a bowl, if using a stick blender) and blitz until smooth.

Transfer the ice cream to the lidded freezer-proof container and place it back into the freezer until shortly before you are ready to serve. It will keep well for up to 2–3 months in the freezer.

Remove the ice cream from the freezer 10 minutes before serving, to let it soften a little. Serve topped with the blueberry gin.

SWAP THIS: This ice cream can be made with any frozen fruit as long as you use the frozen bananas as well.

TIP: Use bananas with very spotted skins to ensure that they are sweet.

APPLE *and* APRICOT
OATY CRUMBLE

🕐 **15 MINS**   🍲 **55 MINS**   🍴 **SERVES 6**

PER SERVING:
246 KCAL / 36G CARBS

4 cooking apples, approximately
  500g, peeled, cored and thinly
  sliced
1 x 411g tin apricot halves, drained
25g white granulated sweetener
grated zest of ½ lemon
150g plain flour
75g reduced-fat spread
50g oats
30g brown granulated sweetener
¼ tsp ground cinnamon

TO ACCOMPANY *(optional)*
Custard, page 245 (+ 58 kcal
  per serving)

This fruity crumble is so easy to prepare and combines fresh apples and tinned apricots with a lightly spiced, oaty topping. We've reduced the amount of calories in the crumble topping by using reduced-fat spread and brown sweetener, to create a dessert that's low on calories, but big on flavour. Super fruity and warming, this dish is perfect for those cooler evenings! Try serving it with our easy peasy Custard on page 245.

Special Occasion

Preheat the oven to 200°C (fan 180°C/gas mark 6).

Mix together the apples, apricots, white sweetener and lemon zest. Place in an 18cm x 27cm (roughly 7in x 10½in) ovenproof dish.

Place the flour in a large bowl and add the reduced-fat spread. Rub the reduced-fat spread into the flour until it resembles breadcrumbs. Stir in the oats, brown sweetener and cinnamon.

Spread the oat mixture over the apples and apricots and place the dish on a baking tray. Place in the preheated oven and bake for 50–55 minutes, until the fruit is tender and the topping is golden. (Or you can cool and freeze to have later.)

TIP: Make sure that the tinned apricots are well drained, otherwise the cooked fruit mixture may be too wet.

CUSTARD

⏱ **5 MINS** 🍲 **15 MINS** ✕ **SERVES 6**

PER SERVING:
58 KCAL / 5.8G CARBS

375ml skimmed milk
2 egg yolks
1½ tsp vanilla extract
1 tbsp cornflour
3 tbsp granulated sweetener

Packet mixes be gone, this custard recipe is low on calories, super tasty and ready in a jiffy! It's delicious when served with pretty much any pud, but we think that it works especially well with our Apple and Apricot Oaty Crumble or our Spotted Dick (see pages 242 and 248). If you love your custard really thick then just add an extra tablespoon of cornflour to your mix, but don't forget to adjust the calories accordingly!

Weekly Indulgence ─────────────

Pour the milk into a large saucepan. Heat over a medium heat until it just starts to steam, but be careful not to let it boil or burn on the bottom of the pan.

While the milk heats up, put all of the other custard ingredients in a heatproof jug and mix thoroughly to form a smooth paste.

Once the milk is steaming, pour it into the jug and mix quickly with the eggs and other ingredients. Pour the mixture back into the saucepan.

Return the saucepan to a medium heat and cook slowly, stirring with a whisk, for 5–10 minutes. It will start to thicken gradually. Resist the urge to turn the heat up high as this can cause the custard to split or burn on the bottom of the pan, and make sure you stir continuously. Once the custard gently starts to 'blip' and bubble, it is ready! Leave it to stand for a minute before serving.

CHURROS *and* CHOCOLATE SAUCE

🕐 **5 MINS** 📦 **25 MINS** ✕ **SERVES 6**

PER SERVING:
178 KCAL /14G CARBS

1½ tbsp brown granulated
  sweetener
55g unsalted reduced-fat butter
125ml water
¼ tsp salt
90g plain flour
½ tsp vanilla extract
1 egg
1 tbsp granulated sweetener
1 tsp ground cinnamon
60ml reduced-fat cream
  alternative
50g dark chocolate, broken
  into pieces

Inspired by the classic Spanish dessert, our lighter version of this dish uses a few clever swaps to keep the calories low without compromising on flavour. Served with a rich, chocolate dipping sauce, these churros are perfect for sharing and can also be easily reheated the next day to help curb your chocolate cravings!

Everyday Light ───────────────

Preheat the oven to 220°C (fan 200°C/gas mark 7).

In a small saucepan combine the brown granulated sweetener, reduced-fat butter, water and salt. Heat slowly over a medium heat until the butter has melted. Bring to the boil and take off the heat. Tip in the flour and beat until it forms a ball and comes away from the sides of the pan. Add the vanilla extract and egg. The mixture will look like it has separated at first, but carry on mixing and it will come back together and turn glossy.

Line two baking sheets with greaseproof paper and pour the mixture into a piping bag fitted with a star-shaped nozzle. It's sometimes best to fill the bag with half the mixture at a time so that it isn't too full and difficult to handle when piping the churro shapes. Pipe thirty churros, approximately 10cm (4in) in length, onto the baking sheets, leaving room for them to spread slightly. Bake in the oven for 20 minutes until they are crispy and golden brown in colour.

Mix the sweetener and ground cinnamon in a small bowl and dip each churro in the mix, coating them on all sides. Leave them on the baking sheets and keep warm in the oven.

Add the cream to a small pan and slowly bring to the boil. Take off the heat and tip the chocolate into the pan, stirring until glossy and combined.

Pour the sauce into a small bowl and serve with the warm churros.

TIP: Leaving your churros in the oven with the door ajar for 5 minutes before dipping in the cinnamon and sweetener mix gives the churros a really crispy outer edge, which means you can load them with more chocolate sauce.

SPOTTED DICK

🕐 **10 MINS** 🍲 **55 MINS** ✕ **SERVES 4**

PER SERVING:
285 KCAL / 37G CARBS

150g plain flour
2 tsp baking powder
pinch of salt
¼ tsp mixed spice
75g reduced-fat spread, plus
    a little extra for greasing
40g raisins
2 tbsp brown granulated
    sweetener
finely grated zest of ½ lemon
100ml semi-skimmed milk

TO ACCOMPANY *(optional)*
Custard, page 245 (+ 58 kcals
    per serving)

A low-calorie version of the classic British pudding, 'spotted' with raisins and flavoured with a hint of lemon and mixed spice. This is comfort food at its finest: warming and filling, and delicious served with custard.

Special Occasion ———————————

Preheat the oven to 190°C (fan 170°C/gas mark 5).

Thoroughly grease a 1-litre ovenproof pudding basin. Place a greased disc of greaseproof paper in the bottom of the basin. Sift together the flour, baking powder, salt and mixed spice in a medium bowl. Add the reduced-fat spread and rub into the flour mixture until it resembles breadcrumbs. Stir in the raisins, sweetener and lemon zest. Add the milk and stir in using a round-bladed knife until well combined. Scrape into the prepared pudding basin and level the surface.

Place a disc of greased greaseproof paper on the surface of the pudding. This should be large enough to cover the whole surface. Cut a circle of foil to cover the top of the pudding. This should overlap the rim of the pudding basin by about 5cm (2in) all the way round.

Fold the foil down around the whole pudding basin and secure by tying with string around the rim.

Place in the oven and bake for 50–55 minutes, or until cooked. Test to see if the pudding is cooked by inserting a small sharp knife into the centre. The knife will come out clean when the pudding is cooked.

Remove from the oven and remove the foil lid and the greaseproof paper. Turn out onto a serving plate and remove the disc of greaseproof paper. Serve at once.

TIP: Make sure the pudding basin is thoroughly greased and lined with a disc of greased greaseproof paper, otherwise the pudding might stick to the bowl.

LEMON SURPRISE PUDDING

🕐 **10 MINS**   🍲 **40 MINS**   ✕ **SERVES 6**

PER SERVING:
235 KCAL / 26G CARBS

75g reduced-fat spread, plus a
  little extra for greasing
85g caster sugar
85g white granulated sweetener
grated zest and juice of 3 lemons
3 egg yolks
75g self-raising flour
250ml semi-skimmed milk
3 egg whites
¼ tsp icing sugar, for dusting

A light, fluffy pudding that separates during baking to produce an airy sponge on the top and a moist, lemon sauce underneath. This dessert is full of zingy citrus flavours and is so easy to make – perfect for a midweek treat! As this pudding produces its own sauce, it doesn't need to be served with any other sauces or custard. Guaranteed to become a new, firm favourite!

Weekly Indulgence

Preheat the oven to 180°C (fan 160°C/gas mark 4).

Grease a 1.3-litre ovenproof dish with a little reduced-fat spread. Place the reduced-fat spread, caster sugar, sweetener and lemon zest in a large bowl and beat using an electric whisk for 2–3 minutes until creamed together. Add the lemon juice, egg yolks, flour and milk, then mix until smooth.

Place the egg whites in a large bowl. Wash the whisk heads in hot, soapy water and dry well. Whisk the egg whites until they form soft peaks. Using a large metal spoon, carefully fold the whisked egg whites into the flour mixture until just combined. Take care not to over mix, otherwise you may knock out the air. Tip the mixture into the prepared ovenproof dish.

Place in the preheated oven and bake for 35–40 minutes until golden. The pudding will be slightly wobbly in the centre.

Remove from the oven and leave to stand for 10 minutes before serving. Dust the top with the icing sugar and serve.

TIP: Make sure that the whisk heads and bowl are really clean and free from grease otherwise the egg whites may not stiffen when whisked.

CINNAMON SWIRLS

 10 MINS   **20 MINS**   ✕ **MAKES 32**

PER SERVING:
34 KCAL / 3.9G CARBS

320g light puff pastry
1 tsp cold water
2 tbsp granulated sweetener
2 tsp ground cinnamon
1 tsp skimmed milk

TO ACCOMPANY *(optional)*
serve with a scoop of low-calorie ice cream (+ about 78 kcal per serving). Calories will vary depending on the ice cream brand used.

Packed full of warming, sweet cinnamon, these tasty pastries are perfect with a cuppa on a chilly afternoon. They also work really well when served as a dessert alongside some low-calorie ice cream or even as a cheeky breakfast treat! Why not play around with different spices? Some ground ginger or mixed spice would also work really well!

Everyday Light ─────────────────────

Preheat the oven to 190°C (fan 170°C/gas mark 5) and line a baking tray with baking parchment.

Unroll the pastry and moisten with the cold water. Sprinkle over the granulated sweetener, followed by the cinnamon to form an even layer. Roll the pastry along the long edge, to form a long roll. Try to keep the roll as tight as possible. Use a little water along the far edge to help the roll stick together.

Cut into thirty-two pieces – a bread knife is good for this – and place each swirl onto the baking tray. Press each swirl down a little to help the pastry layers stick together.

Brush each swirl with a little milk and bake for 20 minutes until crisp and golden.

Leave to cool on a wire rack and enjoy! You can also freeze the swirls to have later.

PORTUGUESE CUSTARD TARTS

🕐 **5 MINS**　🍲 **20 MINS**　✗ **SERVES 12**

PER SERVING:
66 KCAL / 6G CARBS

low-calorie cooking spray
170g light puff pastry (use a
　standard-size sheet, each cut
　circle should weigh around 14g)
1 large egg
1 large egg yolk
100ml skimmed milk
4 tbsp gold granulated
　sweetener or any other natural,
　granulated sweetener
1 tsp ground nutmeg

Inspired by the traditional Portuguese *Pastéis de nata*, our take on this dish uses reduced-fat puff pastry to help keep the calories low. The creamy egg custard filling is flavoured with a sprinkle of nutmeg to help these tarts pack a flavour punch – perfect for enjoying as part of a dessert or with an afternoon cuppa!

Everyday Light ─────────────────────

Preheat the oven to 190°C (fan 170°C/gas mark 5). Spray a mini muffin tray with low-calorie cooking spray.

Unroll the puff pastry. Using a cutter which is slightly larger than each muffin dip, cut twelve circles. Place each pastry circle into the mini muffin tray, pushing carefully into the sides.

Mix the egg, egg yolk, milk and sweetener in a jug – make sure you whisk until it is fully combined so there is no separation in the egg. Pour into each pastry case.

Sprinkle each custard tart with a little ground nutmeg and bake in the oven for 20 minutes, until the pastry is golden and the egg is just set.

Remove from the oven, take out of the tray and leave to cool on a wire rack before serving. (You could also freeze them to have another day.)

NUTRITIONAL INFO PER SERVING

Breakfast	ENERGY KJ/KCAL	FAT (G)	SATURATED FAT (G)	CARBS (G)	SUGAR (G)	FIBRE (G)	PROTEIN (G)
LOTUS BISCOFF AMERICAN PANCAKES	1285/307	15	3.6	29	11	2.8	12
BANANA DIPPERS	1342/318	7.8	1.9	49	28	3.1	11
JAMMY DODGER FRENCH TOAST	1148/273	7	1.8	35	13	6.9	14
BUBBLE AND SQUEAK	859/203	2.1	0.4	32	5.3	5	12
DILL, CREAM CHEESE AND SMOKED SALMON BAGEL	971/231	7.6	3.6	27	4.9	3.2	13
BREAKFAST POTATOES	845/200	0.8	0.2	40	12	7.2	5
SQUASHAGE FINGERS	1445/344	10	3.6	23	3.1	8	35
CHOCOLATE BANANA MUFFINS	628/149	2.4	0.9	26	12	2.5	4.5

FAKEAWAYS	ENERGY KJ/KCAL	FAT (G)	SATURATED FAT (G)	CARBS (G)	SUGAR (G)	FIBRE (G)	PROTEIN (G)
THAI BASIL CHICKEN	1014/240	2.4	0.5	17	12	5.8	35
CHAR SIU PORK BURGERS	1344/319	7.9	2.7	25	4.4	4.9	34
TERIYAKI CHICKEN	1318/311	2.5	0.6	32	29	5.2	37
TEX-MEX MEATBALLS	1616/383	6.7	1.6	31	17	11	42
PORK LARB LETTUCE WRAPS	793/189	6.5	2.4	2.9	2.1	1.7	28
CHICKEN AND BANANA CURRY	1457/346	9.4	1	24	18	3.9	39
BAKED CHIMICHANGA	1706/405	7.1	3.5	45	16	15	31
CREAMY LENTIL DHAL	879/208	2.3	0.8	31	8.5	4.8	12
VEGGIE SATAY NOODLES	1299/308	4.3	0.8	46	13	9.2	13
CREAMY VEGETABLE PANANG CURRY	1105/264	8.8	1.4	23	15	9	18
SWEDISH MEATBALLS	1531/365	15	5.5	12	3.8	2.2	45
CHICKEN AND PINEAPPLE STIR-FRY	891/211	2	0.5	14	13	3.6	31

FAKEAWAYS	ENERGY KJ/KCAL	FAT (G)	SATURATED FAT (G)	CARBS (G)	SUGAR (G)	FIBRE (G)	PROTEIN (G)
CHICKEN SHASHLIK	1011/239	2.8	0.7	9.2	7	3.8	42
HONEY CHILLI PORK	1191/282	5.3	2	13	11	1.3	45
CRISPY CHILLI BEEF	1464/349	15	5.9	20	11	3.4	31
A CHICKEN'S VINDALOO	1407/335	11	3.1	24	17	7.1	29
ZINGY CHICKEN SALAD	889/211	5.2	1.1	6.9	0.7	1.2	33
STIR-FRIED BEEF WITH GINGER AND SPRING ONIONS	1294/309	13	5.5	15	9.5	4.1	30
CHINESE CHICKEN AND BROCCOLI	778/184	2.4	0.5	16	9.7	6.1	22
SPICY RICE	1680/397	2.4	0.5	82	4	4.1	9.7
CHICKEN CHOW MEIN	1518/359	2.7	0.6	45	15	9.6	33

BATCH COOK	ENERGY KJ/KCAL	FAT (G)	SATURATED FAT (G)	CARBS (G)	SUGAR (G)	FIBRE (G)	PROTEIN (G)
CREAMY BOLOGNESE	1307/310	8.2	3.9	20	17	5.8	36
CREAMY CHICKEN AND TARRAGON HOTPOT	1569/371	3.7	0.8	42	11	7	40
CHICKEN MARSALA	833/198	6.3	2.1	7.3	1.9	1.1	28
CHICKEN CHASSEUR	1392/330	5.3	1	16	13	6.3	50
PULLED CHICKEN BAKED SLIDERS	1247/296	6.1	2.1	34	8.2	5.3	23
SALISBURY STEAK	1151/274	8.5	3.3	16	5.6	3.1	32
MONGOLIAN BEEF	2104/500	14	4.5	23	12	3.6	69
DIJON PORK	1348/320	8.1	2.9	10	5.4	2.2	51
PEPPERCORN CHICKEN	815/193	3	0.9	2.7	1.9	0.6	38
PIZZA PASTA	1643/390	11	4.7	48	14	6.6	20
PHILLY CHEESESTEAK MEATLOAF	1537/366	12	4.3	18	10	4	45
CREAMY TUSCAN CHICKEN	1114/264	4.5	1.6	13	11	3.7	39

BATCH COOK	ENERGY KJ/KCAL	FAT (G)	SATURATED FAT (G)	CARBS (G)	SUGAR (G)	FIBRE (G)	PROTEIN (G)
CHEESEBURGER QUICHE	1195/285	12	5.8	9.7	8.2	2.1	32
CREAMY CAJUN CHICKEN PASTA	1999/474	8.1	2.6	60	16	10	35
SAUSAGE CASSEROLE	1968/468	12	3.4	60	23	13	22
MUSHY PEA CURRY	1337/317	3	0.6	34	11	11	33
BOLOGNESE RISOTTO	1409/333	4.5	1.7	46	14	6.2	21

STEWS & SOUPS	ENERGY KJ/KCAL	FAT (G)	SATURATED FAT (G)	CARBS (G)	SUGAR (G)	FIBRE (G)	PROTEIN (G)
CHICKEN TORTILLA SOUP	1562/370	5.4	1.3	39	16	12	34
HERBY CHICKEN STEW WITH DUMPLINGS	1593/378	5.8	1.3	48	6.9	7.8	30
MALAYSIAN FISH CURRY	1292/306	5.7	1.6	27	6.5	5.3	34
MUSHRROOM BOURGUIGNON	820/195	2	0.2	28	19	8.5	11
MEXICAN STREET CORN SOUP	838/199	4.4	1.5	28	12	6.4	8.5
VEGETARIAN GUMBO	604/144	2.1	0.3	19	14	8.3	6.9
LENTIL AND BACON SOUP	1001/237	2.8	0.5	32	6.3	5.4	18
BROCCOLI AND CHEDDAR SOUP	662/158	5.6	3.2	15	3.9	4.3	9.7
CARIBBEAN VEGETABLE STEW	1377/327	4	1.4	55	25	14	10

BAKES & ROASTS	ENERGY KJ/KCAL	FAT (G)	SATURATED FAT (G)	CARBS (G)	SUGAR (G)	FIBRE (G)	PROTEIN (G)
PORK AND APPLE TRAYBAKE	1296/308	6.2	2	26	19	7.9	33
VIKING PORK	1360/325	15	7.6	3.8	2.6	0.8	43
HONEY AND LIME SALMON	1181/283	18	3.3	4.1	3.5	0.5	25
DIRTY MACARONI	1158/275	7.2	3	24	8.9	4.4	25

BAKES & ROASTS	ENERGY KJ/KCAL	FAT (G)	SATURATED FAT (G)	CARBS (G)	SUGAR (G)	FIBRE (G)	PROTEIN (G)
HARISSA AND HONEY CHICKEN	1831/435	9.7	2.5	27	24	7.8	54
CHICKEN POT PIE CRUMBLE	2130/505	11	3	56	8.8	8.7	42
VEGETABLE AND CHICKPEA ROAST	796/190	5.9	2	20	5.6	6.5	11
LAMB, ROSEMARY AND SWEET POTATO PIE	1432/340	9	3.7	40	16	6.3	21
STEAK DIANE	1297/309	11	5	2.7	1.3	0.6	49
FILO FISH PIE	1342/318	4.4	1.4	26	8.4	3.7	42
TUNA MELT PEPPERS	1023/243	7.8	4.4	21	8.5	3.3	20
CORNED BEEF HASH PATTIES	908/216	6.6	3	20	3.8	3.4	18
CREAMY CHICKEN PASTA BAKE	2137/506	10	4.7	56	5.3	4.6	45
SUMMER VEGETABLE RISOTTO	1493/353	4.6	1.8	63	3.4	4.4	12
FALAFEL TRAYBAKE	1207/286	2.8	0.4	51	22	11	8.3
CHEESY BROCCOLI STUFFED CHICKEN	827/196	5.1	2.8	3.5	2.6	2.2	33
CHIMICHURRI LAMB CHOPS	977/235	19	8.6	1.4	0.5	0.6	15
CHEESY VEGETABLE PIE	2453/585	25	15	55	11	4.9	34
CRUSTLESS QUICHE LORRAINE	1404/336	19	8.2	6.2	4.7	2.8	34
CHICKEN KIEVS	1121/268	8.9	2.6	9.9	1.2	1.9	37
TOAD-IN-THE-HOLE	1497/355	8.6	2.3	37	8.8	5.5	30

SNACKS AND SIDES	ENERGY KJ/KCAL	FAT (G)	SATURATED FAT (G)	CARBS (G)	SUGAR (G)	FIBRE (G)	PROTEIN (G)
LEMON AND GARLIC ASPARAGUS	169/40	0.8	0.1	3.1	2.6	2.2	3.9
BOMBAY POTATOES	707/167	1	0.1	32	6.3	5.1	4.7
LYONNAISE POTATOES	1077/255	1.3	0.1	51	6.9	6.7	6.4
COBB SALAD	1537/368	18	5.5	11	6.8	4.1	38

SNACKS AND SIDES	ENERGY KJ/KCAL	FAT (G)	SATURATED FAT (G)	CARBS (G)	SUGAR (G)	FIBRE (G)	PROTEIN (G)
CAULIFLOWER CHEESE AND POTATO MASH	1045/248	7.3	4.3	32	3.2	4.2	4
LIME AND COCONUT JASMINE RICE	992/234	1.4	1	50	2	1	4.9
BOMBAY CHICKPEAS	327/78	2	0.2	9.2	0.5	2.8	4.4
SIMPLE NAAN BREAD	1178/278	3.3	0.8	52	6.4	2.5	9.4
BRAISED RED CABBAGE	366/87	0.9	0	14	12	5.7	2.4
COLESLAW	337/80	0.8	0	12	11	5.2	3.6
ORZO PRIMAVERA PASTA SALAD	902/213	1.2	0.2	41	3.9	2.3	8
BEETROOT AND MINT HUMMUS	659/156	0.6	0	22	3.3	9	9.9

Sweet treats	ENERGY KJ/KCAL	FAT (G)	SATURATED FAT (G)	CARBS (G)	SUGAR (G)	FIBRE (G)	PROTEIN (G)
BAILEYS CHOCOLATE CHEESECAKE POTS	452/108	4.7	2.9	5.8	5.3	0.5	8.7
CHOCOLATE TARTS	308/74	4.3	2.1	6.3	1.3	0.5	2.2
SALTED CARAMEL RICE KRISPIE BARS	483/115	3.1	1.7	20	0.5	0.5	1
SWEET POTATO BROWNIES	402/96	5.3	1.6	8.8	1.8	1.1	2.6
PINEAPPLE WITH LIME AND CINNAMON	384/91	0.5	0	18	17	3.5	0.7
BLUEBERRY, GIN AND BANANA ICE CREAM	412/98	0.5	0	18	12	3	1.1
APPLE AND APRICOT OATY CRUMBLE	1032/246	8.7	2	36	11	3.7	4
CUSTARD	243/58	2.1	0.6	5.8	3	0	3.2
CHURROS AND CHOCOLATE SAUCE	743/178	11	5.4	14	2.8	1.9	3.8
SPOTTED DICK	1196/285	13	3.1	37	8.3	2.2	4.9
LEMON SURPRISE PUDDING	986/235	12	3.1	26	17	0.9	5.9
CINNAMON SWIRLS	141/34	1.7	0.9	3.9	0	0.5	0.6
PORTUGUESE CUSTARD TARTS	278/66	3.7	1.7	6	0.5	0.5	2.1

ACCOMPANIMENTS	ENERGY KJ/KCAL	FAT (G)	SATURATED FAT (G)	CARBS (G)	SUGAR (G)	FIBRE (G)	PROTEIN (G)
MIXED SALAD (75G)	64/15	0.5	0.1	1.5	1.1	0.9	1.1
STEAMED VEGETABLES (80G)	160/38	0.5	0.1	5	2.8	1.9	2.7
COOKED NEW POTATOES (3 MEDIUM/126G)	353/83	0	0	17	1.4	2.3	2.3
BABY NEW POTATOES (160G)	448/106	0	0	22	1.7	2.9	2.9
STEAMED CARROTS (90G)	133/32	0.5	0.1	5.2	4.8	2.5	0.5
BAKED POTATO (225G UNCOOKED)	697/165	0.5	0.2	24	2.3	4.3	4.1
50G UNCOOKED PASTA	737/174	1	0.1	34	1.6	2.5	6
BASMATI RICE (50G DRY/125G COOKED)	737/173	0.5	0.1	38	0	0.5	4.3
FINELY GRATED PARMESAN (15.5G)	257/62	4.5	2.9	0	0	0	5.3
EGG FRIED IN LOW-CALORIE COOKING SPRAY	421/101	6.9	1.9	0	0	0	9.6
POACHED EGG	309/74	5.3	1.5	0	0	0	6.7
¼ SLICED AVOCADO (35G)	285/69	6.8	1.4	0.7	0	1.2	0.7
THINLY SLICED CUCUMBER (35G)	23/6	0.5	0	0.5	0.5	0.5	0.5
LOW-CALORIE TORTILLA WRAP (40G)	441/104	0.5	0.3	21	1.4	2.8	3
WHOLEMEAL ROTI (40G)	441/104	0.5	0.3	21	1.4	2.8	3
WHOLEMEAL BREAD ROLL (60G)	644/152	2	0.5	25	1.5	3.3	6.8
LOW-CALORIE/VIRTUALLY FAT-FREE ICE CREAM	330/78	0.6	0	15	14	0	3.2
FAT-FREE GREEK YOGHURT (50G)	123/29	0	0	2	2	0	5.3

BAKES
&
ROASTS

SNACKS
and
SIDES

Sweet
treats

INDEX

leeks
  broccoli and Cheddar soup 148, *149*
  cheesy vegetable pie 190, *190*
  filo fish pie *174*, 175
  herby chicken stew with dumplings 132–3, *134–5*
lemons 14
  lemon and garlic asparagus 200, *201*
  lemon surprise pudding 250, *251*
lentils
  creamy lentil dhal 58, *59*
  lentil and bacon soup *146*, 147
lettuce: pork larb lettuce wraps 52, *53*
limes 14
  honey and lime salmon 158, *159*
  lime and coconut Jasmine rice 212, *213*
  pineapple with lime and cinnamon 236, *237*
Lotus Biscoff American pancakes 24, *25*
low-calorie spray 15
Lyonnaise potatoes 204, *205*

M

macaroni, dirty 160, *161*
Malaysian fish curry 136, *137*
mangetout: chicken chow mein 86, *87*
maple syrup: chocolate banana muffins 40, *41*
Marsala wine: chicken Marsala 94, *95*
meatballs
  Swedish meatballs 66, *67*
  Tex-Mex meatballs 50, *51*
meatloaf, Philly cheesesteak 114, *115*
Mexican street corn soup 140, *141*
mint
  beetroot and mint hummus *224*, 225
  chimichurri lamb chops 188, *189*
Mongolian beef *104*, 105
muffins, chocolate banana 40, *41*
mushrooms
  chicken chasseur *96*, 97
  chicken Marsala 94, *95*
  Chinese chicken and broccoli 82, *83*
  creamy chicken pasta bake *180*, 181
  Dijon pork 106, *107*
  lamb, rosemary and sweet potato pie *170*, 171
  mushroom bourguignon *138*, 139
  Philly cheesesteak meatloaf 114, *115*
  Salisbury steak 100–3, *101*
  steak Diane *172*, *173*
  stir-fried beef with ginger and spring onion 80, *81*

vegetarian gumbo 144, *145*
mushy pea curry 124, *125*
mustard: Dijon pork 106, *107*

N

naan bread, simple *216*, 217
noodles
  chicken chow mein 86, *87*
  veggie satay noodles 62, *63*
nutritional info 256–61

O

oats: apple and apricot oaty crumble 242, *243*
oils: low-calorie spray 15
onions
  breakfast potatoes 36, *37*
  a chicken's vindaloo 76, *77*
  Thai basil chicken 44, *45*
orzo primavera pasta salad 222, *223*
oyster sauce: char siu pork burgers 46, 47

P

pak choi
  slaw 46, *47*
  veggie satay noodles 62, *63*
panang curry, creamy vegetable 64, *65*
pancakes, Lotus Biscoff American 24, *25*
parsley
  chimichurri lamb chops 188, *189*
  dirty macaroni 160, *161*
parsnips: pork and apple traybake 154, *155*
pasta
  creamy Bolognese 90, *91*
  creamy Cajun chicken pasta 120, *121*
  creamy chicken pasta bake 180, *181*
  dirty macaroni 160, *161*
  orzo primavera pasta salad 222, *223*
  pizza pasta 110, *111*
pastry, ready-made 15
patties
  corned beef hash patties 178, *179*
  Salisbury steak 100–3, *101*
peanut butter powder
  creamy vegetable panang curry 64, *65*
  veggie satay noodles 62, *63*
pearl barley: creamy chicken and tarragon hotpot 92, *93*

ACKNOWLEDGEMENTS

We owe a million thank yous to so many people for all their support throughout the creation of this book.

We want to say a huge thank you, firstly, to all of our followers on social media and all those who continue to make our recipes and let us know what they want next! We're so proud that Pinch of Nom has helped, and continues to help, so many people.

Thank you to our publisher Carole Tonkinson. To Martha Burley, Isabel Hewitt, Bríd Enright, Jodie Mullish, Sian Gardiner, Laura Nickoll, Jess Duffy, Zainab Dawood and the rest of the team at Bluebird for helping us create this book and believing in Pinch of Nom enough for there to be a THIRD book! Major thanks also to our agent Clare Hulton for your unwavering support and guidance.

To Mike English for the ace photos and to Kate Wesson for making our food look so, so good. Big thanks go out to Nikki Dupin and Emma Wells of studio Nic&Lou for making this book so beautiful! A special shout-out to Mel Four at Bluebird for creating the beautiful cover.

We also want to thank our friends and family who have made this book possible. Special thanks to Laura Davis and Katie Mitchell for the endless hours you've put into this and for working so hard to get things right! Additional thanks to Matthew Maney, Stephen Milns, Rubi Bourne, Vince Bourne and Cheryl Lloyd for supporting us and the business – we are so proud to work alongside you all. Thanks also to Sophie Fryer, Ellie Owen, Nicola Dales and Mollie Davies for your writing and marketing support.

To our wonderful moderators and online support team; thank you for all your hard work keeping the peace and for all your support.

A huge thank you to our wonderful recipe development team who work tirelessly to help us bring these recipes to life: Lisa Allinson, Cate Meadows, Sharon Fitzpatrick, Steve Cowderoy and Holly Levell.

Furry thanks to Ginger Cat, Freda and Brandi for the daily moments of joy.

And finally... Huge thanks go to Paul Allinson for your unwavering support. And to Cath Allinson who is never forgotten.

ABOUT THE AUTHORS

KATE *and* KAY

Founders of Pinch of Nom
www.pinchofnom.com

Kate Allinson and Kay Featherstone owned a restaurant together on the Wirral, where Kate was head chef. Together they created the Pinch of Nom blog with the aim of teaching people how to cook. They began sharing healthy, slimming recipes and today Pinch of Nom is the UK's most visited food blog with an active and engaged online community of over 1.6 million followers.

Keep on track with the new

PINCH OF NOM FOOD PLANNER: QUICK & EASY

PUBLISHING JUNE 2021